THE
OLD TESTAMENT
FOR A COMPLEX WORLD

THE OLD TESTAMENT FOR A COMPLEX WORLD

How the Bible's Dynamic Testimony
Points to New Life for the Church

Cameron B. R. Howard

Baker Academic
a division of Baker Publishing Group
Grand Rapids, Michigan

Published by Baker Academic
a division of Baker Publishing Group
PO Box 6287, Grand Rapids, MI 49516-6287
www.bakeracademic.com

Printed in the United States of America

Library of Congress Cataloging-in-Publication Data
Names: Howard, Cameron B. R., 1980– author.
Title: The Old Testament for a complex world : how the Bible's dynamic testimony points to new life for the Church / Cameron B.R. Howard.
Description: Grand Rapids, Michigan : Baker Academic, a division of Baker Publishing Group, [2021] | Includes bibliographical references and index
Identifiers: LCCN 2020047764 | ISBN 9781540963727 (paperback) | ISBN 9781540964274 (casebound)
Subjects: LCSH: Bible. Old Testament—Criticism, interpretation, etc. | Bible. Old Testament—Language, style. | Bible—Evidences, authority, etc. | Church renewal.
Classification: LCC BS1171.3 .H69 2021 | DDC 221.6—dc23
LC record available at https://lccn.loc.gov/2020047764

21 22 23 24 25 26 27   7 6 5 4 3 2 1

For Cader

Contents

Acknowledgments

The idea for this book emerged from a workshop I led some years ago at Luther Seminary's Celebration of Biblical Preaching conference. I am grateful to the pastors in that workshop for their generative participation and to the many seminary students who have engaged these ideas with attention, enthusiasm, and patience in my courses over the years.

Luther Seminary's board of trustees granted a year-long sabbatical to work on this project, and I thank them for their ongoing commitment to the flourishing of faculty scholarship for the sake of the church. The support and good cheer of my colleagues in the Bible Division—Michael Chan, David Fredrickson, Rolf Jacobson, Craig Koester, Kathryn Schifferdecker, and Matt Skinner—continue to be a source of great encouragement to me in this and other projects. It is an extraordinary privilege to work with such a talented, collegial group.

It has been a joy to work with the marvelous team at Baker Academic. I am especially grateful for Jim Kinney's sage editorial guidance and Melisa Blok's sharp editorial eye. In a stressful time for the world and on what was, for me, a stressful project, everyone I encountered at Baker was a "non-anxious presence"—a rare gift.

Allen W. Bryan Jr. (MD, PhD) was a delightful conversation partner as I tried to resurrect my long-lost knowledge of physics to describe how biblical interpretation is like an atomic particle collision. I am thankful for his wise counsel and for three decades of friendship.

I finished this book during the pandemic of 2020, when my family and I were at home together all day, every day, for several months. In this way, it feels as if we wrote the book together. Isaac and Anna cheered me on, patiently enduring my absence from their days even though I was just upstairs. And I never could have written this book without the indefatigable support of my husband, Cader, whose wise counsel, love for Christ's church, and commitment always to "make it fun" keep me grounded in hope. I dedicate this book to him.

Abbreviations

General Abbreviations

BCE	before the common era	cf.	confer/compare
ca.	approximately	chap.	chapter
CE	common era	p(p).	page(s)

Old Testament / New Testament

Gen.	Genesis	Neh.	Nehemiah
Exod.	Exodus	Prov.	Proverbs
Lev.	Leviticus	Isa.	Isaiah
Num.	Numbers	Lam.	Lamentations
Deut.	Deuteronomy	Ezek.	Ezekiel
2 Sam.	2 Samuel	Dan.	Daniel
2 Chron.	2 Chronicles	Rev.	Revelation

Apocrypha

1 En.	1 Enoch	2 Macc.	2 Maccabees
1 Macc.	1 Maccabees		

Scripture Versions

AT	author's translation	NRSV	New Revised Standard
CEB	Common English Bible		Version
KJV	King James Version		

Introduction

As I write this introduction, the world is gripped by the coronavirus pandemic. I hope that by the time you read this we will have been released from it, though it is already clear that its effects on our patterns of life will be long-lasting. Every Sunday for the past four months, my husband, a pastor, has broadcast his sermon live from our living room, interspersed with pre-recorded music, liturgy, and prayers. Our ministries of hot meals and fellowship have pivoted to gift cards, Zoom calls, and backyard visits—masked and well-distanced, of course. Denominational bodies and pastoral leaders are debating whether and how the Lord's Supper can be celebrated in online worship services. Every week has brought a new challenge to our assumptions about what the church is, how the church operates, and how the church can adapt to continue making disciples in a very uncertain future. It seems that nothing is the same as it used to be.

In a world that changes by the minute, what good is the study of the Old Testament? We read the Old Testament because it is part of our tradition and because we consider it authoritative, in one way or another. Chances are, though, that we don't flip straight to the Old Testament when we are plotting strategies for the church of the future. After all, these are tumultuous times for religious institutions, even without the disruption wrought by the pandemic. Faced with a narrative of decline fed by financial hardship, steep losses in membership, and diminished cultural status, churches today are looking for a new way forward. Scripture, meanwhile, is iconically *old*. The high school students my brother teaches use the phrase "Bible times" as catch-all slang for anything that seems ancient to them, be it Plato, Shakespeare, or the 1980s. The Bible's chronological and cultural distance from twenty-first-century life lends it authority, on the one hand, but renders it less accessible, on the other. The Old Testament perhaps suffers from this sense of foreignness more than the New Testament; the very title by which it is known within Christianity— *Old* Testament—invites assumptions of its irrelevance. A casual reading of some of its more troubling texts can cement its place as a peculiar artifact of a distant past, even among communities that proclaim the Bible's authority in their lives.

Yet despite its reputation as dusty and strange, the texts of the Old Testament reflect complex, turbulent, and dynamic times for people of faith—times very much like our own. The stories, poems, laws, and prophecies of the Bible came together during political turmoil, theological uncertainty, and intra-community strife—times that required innovation. In this book I hope to show that in today's era of significant cultural upheaval, the Old Testament is of vital importance for the future of the church. The Bible is not a relic of a fizzled faith—quaint and entertaining, perhaps disturbing, but ultimately static and irrelevant. Rather, it is a dynamic collection of texts, representing multiple eras, different voices, and divergent viewpoints. In the ways that those texts often reimagine existing ideas to meet a new day, the Old Testament hosts innovation. By embracing the Old Testament's dynamism, the church is better poised to provide a more holistic biblical foundation for its own days of innovation ahead.

A central claim of this book is that some of the most generative insights for innovation that the Old Testament offers come not only from what it *says*—the words and sentences, stories and poems, and laws and prophecies it contains—but also from *how* those different elements of the Bible came about. Critical biblical scholarship—critical in the sense of *analyzing*, not of *criticizing*—has illuminated the ways that the Old Testament exhibits layers upon layers of composition and editing, which were influenced dramatically by ancient Israel's contact with its neighbors and by its shifting fortunes in the ancient geopolitical landscape. As I endeavor to show the dynamic ethos of the Bible, I will also argue for a more expansive view of biblical authority: one that takes seriously not only the words on those tissue-thin pages but also the circumstances behind their composition. I propose that we consider the Bible as authoritative in its totality, as best as we can know it. That consideration requires studying *how* the Bible says what it says, including the ways in which different perspectives stand side by side, unresolved. The Bible is not authoritative *despite* its diverse voices, its cultural dependencies, and its clashing ideas; rather, the existence of that complexity is part and parcel of its authority.

In this book I propose three modes of innovation that can be gleaned from studying the Old Testament: adapting popular culture, rethinking theological assumptions, and developing a new genre. Chapter 1, "The Bible's Dynamic Witness," highlights five dynamic features inherent in the Bible's composition and content. I argue that by embracing biblical interpretation as a generative, creative process, like so many atoms colliding, the church can better harness the insights of critical biblical scholarship to meet the needs of a changing world. Chapters 2–4 then take deeper dives into the three modes of innovation—that is, three different ways that the texts of the Old Testament point us toward newness and difference as hope-filled possibilities for the future of the church.

Chapter 2, "Adapting Popular Culture," looks at two genres of literature that were widely known in the ancient Near East—flood stories and court tales—and details how the biblical versions of each literary type have been shaped to speak to ancient Israel's particular theological and political concerns. The chapter emphasizes that new circumstances and new experiences can give rise to new methods of storytelling, and it encourages faith communities to reflect on how they are telling their own stories.

Chapter 3, "Rethinking Theological Assumptions," looks at two ways biblical understandings of the community's encounter with God shift over time. In the book of Ezekiel, a shift emerges from the vicissitudes of Israel's political fortunes. In Deuteronomy, a change has likely been crafted to suit a particular agenda. The chapter highlights how different voices in the Old Testament arrive at different conclusions about the same subject, and yet those differing ideas are not erased or smoothed out but instead stand together in the canon. Such dissonances in the text can invite today's churches to consider whether some discordant ideas within faith communities can stand together, unresolved, in life-giving ways.

Chapter 4, "Developing a New Genre," describes how imperial domination of Judah, and particularly the persecutions of Jews by Antiochus IV Epiphanes, gave rise to the peculiar genre of apocalypse, which was both a strategy of survival and a mode of resistance for Jews living in an occupied land under a hostile regime. I argue that the dramatic symbolism of the apocalypse prompts faith communities both to name the oppressive powers that try to claim totalizing control in the world and to look for language that can counteract those powers, offering a vision of an alternate reality.

The final chapter, "Biblical Foundations for Creative Change," offers concluding reflections in the form of basic biblical principles for creative change in communities of faith. The insights of biblical scholarship point to a tradition that values multiple voices and innovative responses to changing political, cultural, and theological circumstances, even as it maintains fidelity to the God of Israel. As churches navigate a changing world, the Old Testament offers new possibilities for a way forward.

It must be emphasized up front that neither the Bible nor this book provides a step-by-step guide for how churches should position themselves for the future. I do not claim that the church should—or even could—replicate the modes of innovation that I identify within the Old Testament. Every community has its own context to navigate. This book is, at its core, a book about the Bible, not a book about church leadership. Nevertheless, biblical studies has much to offer conversations on ecclesial transformation. The Old Testament witnesses to the dynamism inherent in humanity's attempts to live faithfully under God. Studying the Bible in all its fullness shows us that strategic change has always been part of the life of faith, and hope for the future can be found even in the most ancient corners of our tradition.

1

The Bible's Dynamic Witness

And why is that important for the church?"
I was at a dinner with colleagues when the retired seminary president sitting next to me asked for a synopsis of my recently completed dissertation. Like any emerging scholar, I was accustomed to that request, and I had developed a well-rehearsed speech of about three sentences that nicely encapsulated the project's central question and the argument I was making in response to it. I gave a succinct summary of the Persian Empire's bureaucratic impulses, the biblical texts in which those impulses are either reflected or satirized, and the ways in which my project synthesized methods to illuminate the historical impact of Persia on the literary style of the biblical text.

However, I was not similarly prepared for his follow-up question: "And why is that important for the church?" In fact, I was quite startled by it. I had entered the field of biblical studies because of a deep love for and fascination with the Bible, rooted in my ongoing, lifelong experience of church. In the weekly worship services of my childhood, I would follow along with the Old and New Testament readings in the pew Bible and then keep reading through the rest of the service. Church is where I learned to love the Bible, and I had taken it for granted that any discovery that broadens, however incrementally, our understanding of the biblical text, its backgrounds, or its interpretation through history would by definition be important for the church. Isn't that why we go to seminary—to broaden and deepen our understanding? Isn't that why seminaries hire scholars trained in critical methods of biblical studies to teach their students?

What I began to understand in my conversation with that seminary president, and what I have come to comprehend more fully in the years since, is that while many seminarians and pastors delight in their Bible courses as much as I enjoy teaching them, the connections between "what I learned in seminary" and "what I do every day in church work" are sometimes elusive. Classes in both Old Testament and New Testament richly inform the preaching life of pastors and empower them to teach the Bible well, but the finer points of academic biblical scholarship do not always feel "useful" when pledges are down 20 percent, you have three funeral services to conduct this week, and the machine that folds the bulletins has broken down. Faced with limited time and resources, biblical scholarship can feel like a luxury reserved for flourishes in sermons, rather than a foundational part of the everyday life of the church. That sense of irrelevance can be particularly magnified with regard to the Old Testament, which already struggles under the weight of a rampant, if often unintentional, tendency toward Marcionism in Christian churches. Many Christians regard the Old Testament as boring at best and fearsome, violent, and damaging at worst. It is widely avoided in the pulpit.[1]

Why is critical biblical scholarship important for the church? In this book I will offer an answer to that question by focusing on

1. Many of my seminary students will testify that they have only rarely heard sermons on the Old Testament (or on any text outside of the Gospels) in their local churches, despite the creedal affirmations of the authority of the Old Testament in their denominations. See also the detailed diagnosis, including tallies of Old Testament sermons from popular sources, in Strawn, *Old Testament Is Dying*, 28–38.

the dynamic nature of the Old Testament witness. The many and varied texts of the Bible developed in times of community turmoil, political unrest, and theological uncertainty. In the midst of those unsettled and unsettling contexts, the writers of the Old Testament innovated. They took existing texts, themes, and even theological assumptions and reworked them to meet the needs of a new day. As the world changed around them, they found new ways to tell old stories, and when the facts on the ground challenged core assumptions about how God works in the world, they reoriented themselves to new theological possibilities. In the midst of all the change, one element remained stable: the ongoing relationship between God and Israel, who, despite sprains, strains, and fractures in that relationship, remain tethered together throughout the biblical witness by covenant, ancestral commitments, and sheer tenacity.

Written in Stone

In the book of Exodus, when Moses descends from Mount Sinai after receiving the law from God, he brings with him "the two tablets of the covenant, tablets of stone, written with the finger of God" (Exod. 31:18).[2] The depiction of these stone slabs engraved with the laws of God, by God, is perhaps the most widely recognized representation of a biblical text today. The image of Charlton Heston's Moses cradling the tablets in Cecil B. DeMille's 1956 film *The Ten Commandments* helped to cement their iconic status as a recognizable element of popular culture, not just a symbol within faith communities. Displays of the Ten Commandments on rounded stone slabs continue to dot cities and towns all over the United States, often igniting debates about the separation of church and state and the role of biblical law in the founding of the country.[3]

2. All translations are from the NRSV unless otherwise indicated.
3. For an engaging history of the symbolic power of physical representations of the Ten Commandments in the nineteenth- and twentieth-century United States, see Weissman Joselit, *Set in Stone*.

What do these popular depictions of the Ten Commandments say about the Bible? I will leave for other books the question of what the monuments mean for the relationship between the religious and the secular in the United States. My interest is in how our representations of the Bible and its texts reflect, as well as influence, what we understand the Bible to be. What do these granite renderings communicate about how we regard the Bible, and how do they in turn help to shape our expectations of the Bible when we read it? On purely aesthetic criteria, a monument in stone connotes immovability, steadfastness, and completion—hence the expression "set in stone." Beyond the look and feel of the medium, however, the choice of monumentalizing the Ten Commandments symbolizes a static approach to what is a fundamentally dynamic text.

Listing the commandments communicates that the Bible is full of laws or, more narrowly construed, rules. To be sure, law is a fundamental element of the Hebrew Bible.[4] The relationship between God and Israel is described as a covenant—that is, legal—relationship, and the laws are the stipulations of the covenant. The giving of the law at Sinai is an integral part of the Hebrews' exodus from Egypt, neither separate from it nor incidental to it. Yet this context already alerts us to the fact that the law itself is communicated in a narrative framework, placing its revelation within the broader tale of the Hebrews' enslavement, exodus, wilderness wanderings, and conquest. By no means is law the only genre, or type of text, in the Old Testament. In its pages we find stories, poems, lists, genealogies, and many more genres.

Biblical law itself also contains far more than just the Decalogue.[5] Rabbinic tradition holds that there are 613 commandments

---

4. It is conventional to use the term "Hebrew Bible" in academic settings and "Old Testament" in confessional Christian ones. Given that this book brings together those settings, I will use the two terms interchangeably.

5. "Decalogue," meaning "ten words," is another way to refer to the Ten Commandments. References to the Decalogue in the Torah use the phrase "ten words"

in the Torah, not just ten. The legal material in the Torah also extends beyond absolute prohibitions or commands (known as "apodictic" law) to include case law ("casuistic"), which dominates the Covenant Code, the group of laws in Exodus following the Decalogue (Exod. 20:22–23:19). Casuistic law contains conditional regulations dealing with specific situations; for example, "When individuals quarrel and one strikes the other with a stone or fist so that the injured party, though not dead, is confined to bed, but recovers and walks around outside with the help of a staff, then the assailant shall be free of liability, except to pay for the loss of time, and to arrange for full recovery" (21:18–19). Rather than making sweeping religious or ethical demands, these laws articulate possible situations in the life of the community and suggest just restitutions for victims. Thus the Ten Commandments represent only a sliver of just the legal material, let alone all the material, in the Hebrew Bible. Lifting up the Decalogue as a representation of biblical law, while symbolically effective, can obscure the inherent diversity of the Old Testament corpus.

Furthermore, reifying the commandments in monument form implies that we know exactly what the Ten Commandments are. Usually Exodus 20:1–17 serves as the default list, but in fact there are three places in the Torah where a Decalogue appears, and none is an exact match for another. After Moses descends the mountain with the tablets, he discovers the people in the camp reveling in front of a golden calf that they implored Aaron to construct. Moses is so angry that he throws down the tablets and breaks them (Exod. 32:19). When God instructs Moses to make two new stones for a reissuance of the words of the covenant, the so-called Ritual Decalogue is reported in the text, instead of a repetition of Exodus 20 (34:11–26). Some of the commandments

('aseret haddevarim) rather than "ten commandments" (Exod. 34:28; Deut. 4:13; 10:4).

given here echo Exodus 20—for example, "You shall not make cast idols" (34:17)—but the list is nonetheless markedly different. Furthermore, Exodus 34:27–28 implies that "the words of the covenant, the ten commandments" written on the tablets are this Ritual Decalogue, not the classic formulation found in Exodus 20.[6] Later, Deuteronomy 5 re-presents the Exodus 20 list but with a distinctly Deuteronomic twist: the rationale for keeping the Sabbath is not because God rested on the seventh day but because the Israelites were once slaves in Egypt.

Which of these lists was meant to be on the tablets Moses brought down from the mountain? Or was there something else written on them entirely? If we follow the order of the way things are presented in the text, the first set of tablets could have contained specifications for the tabernacle's construction or even the entirety of the Covenant Code.[7] The issue is complicated further when we consider that different interpretive traditions also number the commandments differently. Even though they all add up to ten, exactly *what* the ten are varies. In Jewish tradition, the first commandment is found in Exodus 20:2—"I am the LORD your God"—which is considered an introductory statement in most Christian renderings and is not counted among the ten. The second commandment in Jewish tradition is then the totality of verses 3–6—no other gods before God, and no fashioning idols. Within Lutheranism, Judaism's second commandment is counted as the first, and then the commandment not to covet (v. 17) is divided into two, so that the numbers still add up to ten. For the Reformed and Anglican traditions, the first commandment is no other Gods, the second is no idols, and the rest align with the Jewish ordering. Inscribing the commandments on stone necessarily asserts one interpretive tradition over the other, even as it obscures the ambiguity present within the biblical text itself.

---

6. Deuteronomy 4:13 and 5:22 specify that the Decalogue (as articulated in Deut. 5:6–21) is written on the tablets.

7. See the discussion in Schniedewind, *How the Bible Became a Book*, 128–34.

Granite renderings of the Ten Commandments imply that the Bible is a static, steady, immovable text, written in stone, presented with clarity and certainty.[8] Even all the "singular" language we use to talk about the Bible—*the* Bible, *the* Word (singular) of God, *Scripture* (as a singular, if also collective, noun)—can direct our attention away from the remarkable diversity of texts, values, possibilities, and proposals contained within it. That is not to say that these ways of describing the Bible are inaccurate or ill advised. On the contrary, reading the Bible in its canonical wholeness is a key part of the Christian interpretive tradition.[9] Nevertheless, language shapes and reinforces how we think. The more we emphasize the singularity of the Bible without acknowledging and affirming the multiplicity within it, the more we risk overlooking elements of Scripture that can broaden and deepen our knowledge of God. This book does not claim that interpretation is an exercise in "relativism," wherein there can be no adjudication between readings. Instead, it is an invitation to allow the dynamism of the Old Testament's witness to be a vital part of the process of interpretation, rather than something smoothed over, corrected, or ignored.

Shifting Metaphors

In seminary we are taught—and rightly so—to conduct exegesis on texts. Exegesis is, simply put, critical analysis, and it can encompass a wide range of methods and approaches. Yet inherent in the etymology of the word "exegesis" is the notion of "drawing out" meaning, as if it might be locked inside the configurations of words and phrases on the page. In my own teaching I have often used the metaphor of "mining" the text for data as one way to

---

8. See Weissman Joselit, *Set in Stone*, 24. Jenna Weissman Joselit points out that, for similar reasons, many nineteenth-century Americans found the Ten Commandments to be "the perfect foundational document" for national identity.

9. See Gignilliat, *Reading Scripture Canonically*.

think about exegesis. Both these concepts rest more or less on the notion that there is some static core of right interpretation buried in every text and that we just need to lasso it with our exegetical ropes and tow it out of its murky depths.

I propose that instead of conceptualizing interpretation as excavation, we think of every encounter between text and reader as an *atomic particle collision*. Atoms—the so-called building blocks of matter—are in constant motion. The more energized they are (for example, by being heated), the faster they move. They can combine with each other to form new molecules, as when two atoms of hydrogen and one atom of oxygen combine to form a water molecule (H_2O). In every chemical reaction, electrons are rearranged and there is a transfer of energy, so that energy is either released or absorbed.[10] In nuclear reactions, an atom's nucleus is changed, and even larger amounts of energy are released.

The aurora borealis, or northern lights, is a popular example of these phenomena. Atomic particles—specifically electrons and protons—are carried from the sun on a strong solar wind to Earth's magnetic field, where they meet molecules of oxygen and nitrogen. The collisions release photons—light energy—in various colors, depending on the molecules involved. We see the results of those collisions in the beauty of the northern lights.

In this analogy, readers and texts are both atomic particles. Like a solar wind, the Holy Spirit energizes the encounter between text and reader. Every encounter thus has the potential to form new molecules of interpretation, releasing energy as light and beauty.

All metaphors are necessarily limited in how much they can accurately convey about the ideas they are trying to communicate,

---

10. These different kinds of chemical reactions are characterized as "endothermic" (absorbing energy) and "exothermic" (releasing energy). For simplicity's sake, I will assume biblical interpretation is an "exothermic" experience. I am grateful to Deborah Gelerter for the conversations that inspired this metaphor and to Dr. Allen Bryan for his help with the scientific explanations. Any remaining errors or shortcomings are entirely my own.

and if we follow this metaphor down into the finer points of physics, we will soon meet the limits of my scientific knowledge.[11] Nevertheless, the notion of biblical interpretation as an atomic particle collision is compelling to me because it emphasizes the explosive, transformative potential of reading Scripture. Every encounter between text and reader is full of energy. This is not—or at least it need not be—an explosion that destroys but rather a generative, life-giving burst. The dynamism of human readers who grow, think, and change is reasonably self-evident, but it is perhaps counterintuitive to think of the Bible "in motion." Yet as our brief look at the Ten Commandments has already shown, it can be quite difficult indeed to "pin down" a biblical text. The Bible is intrinsically dynamic.

In the remainder of this chapter I will highlight a few dynamic features inherent in the Old Testament's history and literature. Then in the chapters that follow I will take a closer look at how that intrinsic dynamism is manifested in three specific types of innovations in the Old Testament—that is, places where a biblical text or group of texts take an existing idea and rethink it to meet new circumstances in a new day. My claim is that these kinds of innovations we observe in the Bible, which are products of its inherent dynamism, can provide hope and inspiration for the church today.

11. When I ran this metaphor by Dr. Allen Bryan—a friend who is a physicist and a physician, as well as an astute theological thinker—he offered this compelling expansion: "In the language of the quantum world, every collision is mediated by a connection shared by those two particles and nothing else. All the connecting particles ("force bosons," particles of fundamental forces) travel at the speed of light—indeed, many connecting particles *are* particles of light (photons). The effects of relativity mean that the connection itself is timeless (infinite time dilation), distance-free (infinite space dilation), private and unique (only the two particles experience it—everyone else only sees the effects), and yet universal (there only being a few kinds of force bosons, it's a shared "experience" all particles encounter). An encounter with the solar wind of Scriptural text, mediated by the ever-present Holy Spirit, brings the reader a timeless, formless moment of insight, changing the direction of the reader's path in a unique yet shared experience." Email correspondence with the author, October 11, 2020.

Features of the Old Testament's Dynamism

Cross-Cultural Influences

The texts of the Hebrew Bible did not arise *ex nihilo*, devoid of any influence from the political, social, and cultural interests of ancient Israel or its surrounding cultures. On the contrary, the texts of the Old Testament reflect the influences of multiple traditions. Ancient Israel was never a people in isolation, and its literary stylings testify to contact with its neighbors. Nestled among powerful empires like Egypt and Assyria, and perched beside the Mediterranean Sea, Israel was well situated for interaction with surrounding civilizations.

Many stories within the Bible itself testify to the frequent movement of people across neighboring territories as a fact of life. Food scarcity is a recurring cause for migration: Famine sends Abraham and Sarah to sojourn in Egypt (Gen. 12:10–20). Later, their great-grandsons will also go to Egypt seeking food, finding their brother Joseph there in the process (Gen. 39–50). In the book of Ruth, famine drives Elimelech and Naomi from Judah to Moab with their two sons, who marry Moabite women: Ruth and Orpah. When food becomes available in Judah again, Naomi and her daughter-in-law Ruth venture back to Bethlehem.

Armed conflict also drove migration into and out of Israel. When Samaria was conquered by the Assyrians in 722 BCE, other subject peoples were settled in the city. The most momentous of the conflicts from the perspective of the biblical authors was the fall of Jerusalem to Babylon in 586 BCE and the concomitant exile of Judah's elites. Around 539 BCE, when Cyrus the Great conquered Jerusalem, the exiles began to return in waves to Judah under Persian rule; the books of Ezra and Nehemiah provide the Bible's primary description of the return. Other exiles remained in Babylon, Egypt, and many other places outside of Judah, so that post-exilic biblical texts reflect experiences of life in Judah under foreign occupation as well as Jewish life in Diaspora.

Cross-cultural contact was not limited to times of catastrophe. Biblical laws protecting the stranger, or sojourner, in the midst of Israel further testify to migration as a basic fact of ancient life. The books of 1 and 2 Kings, which provide accounts of the Israelite monarchy, contain many references to Israel's and Judah's encounters with other nations, both friendly and hostile. For example, King Solomon's wisdom and fame attracted a visit from the queen of Sheba (1 Kings 10:1–10), he traded goods widely with other lands (vv. 11–29), and he made marriage alliances with other nations (11:1–8), much to the chagrin of the Deuteronomistic narrator.

The literary traditions found in the Old Testament are themselves further evidence of cross-cultural contact. Many of the laws in the Covenant Code in Exodus are strikingly similar to laws in cuneiform law collections from Mesopotamia dating from the second millennium BCE. The Code of Hammurabi is a particularly famous example of a law code that closely parallels the Covenant Code as well as predates it. The book of Proverbs has remarkable similarities with the long-standing wisdom tradition of Egypt, including some very close parallels with the "Instruction of Amenemope."[12] The creation and flood accounts in the Primeval History, found in Genesis 1–11, show clear echoes of Mesopotamian myths and epics.[13] While not every parallel between Israelite and other ancient Near Eastern literature indicates literary dependence, the preponderance of similarities again reminds us that Israel was neither self-contained nor isolated but was a vibrant part of the broader ancient Near Eastern culture in which it participated.

Multiple Genres

A useful adage promoted by many biblical scholars is that "the Bible is a library, not a book." Of course, we intuit this whenever

---

12. See Hays, *Hidden Riches*, 297–320.
13. See chap. 2 of this book for a more detailed discussion of these parallels.

we refer to the *books*, plural, of the Bible, and it is clear that each book has different topics and different emphases. But beyond the division of the Old Testament into thirty-nine discrete books, the content of the Bible varies significantly by genre, or type, of literature. The presence of many different kinds of texts invites us to consider how our reading strategies and expectations might shift in accordance with changes in genre.

Even as we just casually flip through the Bible's pages, our eyes might be drawn to the way the layout of a book like Genesis, with predominantly prose sentences that stretch all the way across the page, differs from the layout of a book like Psalms, where the poetic structure of its text creates a lot of blank space in its margins. Those simple variances draw our attention to the presence of many different genres in the Old Testament. Narrative, law, poetry, prose, prophecy, proverbs, folktales, history, autobiography—all these categories and many more can be identified in the Bible.

Often the genre categories for biblical texts overlap; some prophecies are also poems, for example, while other prophetic texts are prose. Any given biblical book can contain multiple genres. Sometimes the genre(s) of a given text is disputed, while other times scholars debate what the constituent features of a genre are.[14] Identifying the genres of biblical texts is not a goal in and of itself, but the assumptions we make about what we are reading can change the kinds of questions we ask as well as tune our ears to different details.

For example, thinking about the book of Esther as a *history* might lead me to investigate whether there is any corroborating evidence outside of the Bible that there was once a Jewish queen of Persia or if any other records survive of the many written edicts referred to in the story. I might also be interested in the way the text depicts life inside the Persian court or the historical relationship

---

14. The question of genre has especially driven the study of apocalyptic literature, which we will consider in detail in chap. 4.

between Diaspora Jews and the Persian Empire. Alternately, thinking about the book of Esther as a *short story* or *novella* might prompt me to reflect on how the text's details contribute to the characterization of its protagonists and antagonists. Noticing that the king has trouble making decisions, doesn't notice details, and revels in excess, I might then look for other elements of *satire* in the story, or I might consider whether satire was a prominent genre in the era of Persian rule. Considering satire could then point me full circle back to questions of the historical relationship between Diaspora Jews and the Persian Empire, to see whether that relationship might prompt satirical depictions of the Persian king.

All these investigations of elements of the book of Esther could lead me to call it a *historical novella* or a *satirical story* or something else entirely. More important than the classification of a biblical book, though, is the way that issues of genre help to illuminate details in the text that might otherwise go uninvestigated. Of course, I will already have used my observations about the text to point me to different genre possibilities; readers move back and forth between text and genre, not simply in one direction. We make decisions about meaning to determine a genre, just as the genre helps us determine meaning.[15] This analytical give-and-take facilitates expansive engagement with the biblical text, investigating texts from different angles and illuminating new possibilities for meaning.

Different Historical Circumstances

The book of Daniel, probably the latest of the Old Testament texts to be written, came together in the middle of the second century BCE. The earliest dates for written biblical texts are more disputed, but many scholars would date the earliest writings to the eighth or seventh century BCE, while others would place them significantly earlier. This means that, at the bare minimum, over

15. Barton, *Reading the Old Testament*, 18.

five hundred years of ancient Israelite history stretch behind the Old Testament books, including significant events that were deeply transformative in the life of the community. That doesn't even count the older, oral traditions that inevitably informed the final written products.

The eighth-century prophet Isaiah navigates the politics of the Syro-Ephraimitic War. Micah, his contemporary, focuses on injustices within Judah inflamed by the pressures of looming international conflict. The searing poetry of the book of Lamentations describes in graphic images the depth of suffering and despair caused by the Babylonian siege of Jerusalem in 586 BCE. Chapters 40–55 of the book of Isaiah include soaring oracles of hope in response to the possibility of a return to Judah under the rule of Cyrus, while Ezra and Nehemiah contemplate the gritty reality of that return a few decades later. Daniel 7–12 reckons with the persecutions of Antiochus IV Epiphanes, which took place in 168–164 BCE. This brief list of examples from the biblical corpus shows how much of the Old Testament literature emerged around various pivot points in the tumultuous history of ancient Israel, providing new responses to changing situations.

One of the challenges the Old Testament presents to interpreters is that the timeline of its composition does not match the timeline presented in its canonical arrangement—that is, the time in which a book was written sometimes differs significantly from the era a book describes. While the Christian canonical ordering of the plotlines of the books from Genesis through 2 Kings is roughly chronological, the development of those books does not similarly align. The book of Ruth, for example, is set "in the days when the judges ruled" (Ruth 1:1a), yet the time of its composition is much later. The text itself testifies to that time difference in how it explains community customs in ways that presume those customs have long-since fallen out of practice (4:7). Not only is dating biblical texts a challenge, but it can also be difficult as a reader to know in what ways the concerns voiced in the stories reflect the historical setting of the stories themselves and in what ways they reflect the concerns of the author's day.

Composite Authorship

If the Bible contains multiple *books* overlapping multiple *genres* and spanning multiple *eras* in the history of ancient Israel, then it will come as no surprise that the Bible's texts were written by multiple *authors*. The scribes responsible for the compilation of 1 and 2 Kings in the sixth or fifth century BCE are obviously not the same people responsible for a second-century text like the book of Daniel. More remarkable is how a single text can show many different compositional hands. The texts of the Pentateuch are perhaps the most famous example of this phenomenon. Broad-based differences in thematic emphasis and theological outlook, coupled with consistent stylistic variations, have led many scholars to see multiple authorial hands at work in the first five books of the Hebrew Bible. The most famous formulation of this idea is the called the Documentary Hypothesis, pioneered by nineteenth-century scholar Julius Wellhausen. Wellhausen proposed that there were four distinct source documents—known as J, E, D, and P—produced at different times in early Israelite history and then pieced together into the final form of the Pentateuch. While the details of the Documentary Hypothesis continue to inspire passionate debate, the general phenomenon of composite author-ship of the Pentateuch, in which multiple strands of tradition have been woven together to produce the text as we know it today, enjoys widespread affirmation.[16]

The story of Balaam and his talking donkey—which has long been one of my favorite biblical tales—serves as an example of composite authorship. At the beginning of Numbers 22, the

---

16. For a helpful primer on major arguments regarding the formation of the Penta-teuch, including the many different trajectories of source criticism since Wellhausen, see Ska, *Introduction to Reading the Pentateuch*.

Israelites are camped in the plains of Moab as they make their way toward Canaan. Moab's King Balak is afraid they are numerous enough to overtake him, so he decides to hire the prophet Balaam from the distant town of Pethor, on the Euphrates, to curse them (Num. 22:1–6). When Balak's emissaries approach Balaam, God appears to Balaam in the night, forbidding him to accompany the officials back to Moab to curse the Israelites. Balak sends a second set of officials, "more numerous and more distinguished than these," to persuade Balaam (v. 15). He initially refuses them, but when God appears to him again at night, this time God grants permission for him to go, as long as he will "do only what I tell you to do" (v. 20). Yet as soon as Balaam leaves, we learn that "God's anger was kindled because he was going, and the angel of the Lord took his stand in the road as his adversary" (v. 22). Why is God mad at Balaam for doing exactly what God has told him to do?

If we are reading synchronically—that is, reading the received form of the text—then these verses introduce some fascinating and eminently worthwhile theological questions about the nature of God's sovereignty and the possibility of divine caprice. This is, without a doubt, a valid and important way to read. If we are reading diachronically, with an eye toward the development of the text over time, then God's odd turnaround here looks like a "seam" in the text: a place where different traditions have been joined together. In fact, Numbers 22:20–21 is part of an editorial feature called "resumptive repetition," which can be identified in many places throughout the Pentateuch. Verse 35 echoes those two introductory verses closely: "The angel of the Lord said to Balaam, 'Go with the men; but speak only what I tell you to speak.' So Balaam went on with the officials of Balak." The story that appears between those lines—the account of Balaam and his talking donkey in verses 22–34—looks like a separately existing story that has been interpolated into the larger Balaam narrative in Numbers 22–24. In the immediate preamble to 22:22–34,

Balaam is surprisingly devoted to the will of the God of Israel, despite not being an Israelite. He is able to receive God's messages successfully and willingly does what God commands. However, in the story in verses 22–34, Balaam cannot see the messenger of God with a drawn sword who stands in the road to oppose him. He is a failed "seer," and his life must be saved by his donkey. Yet as the rest of the narrative continues in chapters 23 and 24, Balaam continues to listen to God and proclaim oracles of blessing for Israel.

We cannot know for certain whether the final author-redactor of Numbers 22–24 had access to the talking donkey episode as a written text composed by a different author or if that was an existing oral tradition worked into the larger narrative by that final redactor. In other words, the language of "composite authorship" might be better understood as "composite traditions," in order to account for the oral layers that surely exist behind the final written form as we have received it.

William M. Schniedewind affirms that "authorship" may not be the best category through which to understand the composition of the Hebrew Bible. The written text of the Bible represents one point on the timeline of a textual tradition that was transmitted orally for centuries before it was ever locked into written form. Schniedewind writes:

> The Classical Hebrew language does not even have a word that means "author." The nearest term would be *sofer*, "scribe," who was a transmitter of tradition and text rather than an author. Authorship is a concept that derives from a predominantly *written* culture, whereas ancient Israelite society was largely an *oral* culture. Traditions and stories were passed on orally from one generation to the next. They had their authority from the *community* that passed on the tradition rather than from an *author* who wrote a text.[17]

17. Schniedewind, *How the Bible Became a Book*, 7.

Whereas today we might think of authorship as a matter of an individual with a copyright, the transmission of oral tradition in ancient Israel was both communal and intergenerational. In her essay on Exodus in *The Africana Bible Commentary*, Judy Fentress-Williams describes the remembering and reshaping of biblical tradition as "remix," a way that "subsequent generations tried to find their way into the narrative."[18] A musical remix highlights certain elements of the original song while also putting a new spin on it. The metaphor of the remix is helpful for exploring the Bible's innovations because a remix brings on change without erasure of the original tradition. Fentress-Williams offers the example of the prophet Amos's recasting of the exodus event at Amos 9:7 to expand the vision of God's saving work: "In this passage, the prophet evokes language and images of God bringing Israel up, used heretofore to express the exclusive nature of Israel's relationship with God to suggest that God's work is not limited to a single people. Moreover, the work of God extends to those previously considered as enemies."[19] The effect of Amos's reemployment of the exodus motif is that a central tradition of the faith is at once reaffirmed and updated.

It is a common impulse to regard critical biblical scholarship as an effort to get back to the "intended meaning" of the text: to recover what its original author(s) meant to say.[20] There are several difficulties with this perspective. First, it presumes we know who the authors are, as well as which part(s) of a given text each person wrote, and that their authorship could be separated from the

---

18. Fentress-Williams, "Exodus," 81.

19. Fentress-Williams, "Exodus," 81.

20. See discussion on "Biblical Criticism and Religious Belief" in Barton, *Nature of Biblical Criticism*, 137–86. The claim to be able to identify the "intent" of a passage is not limited to critical scholarship. Similar language is also wielded by some faith leaders, with or without reference to biblical criticism, to claim absolute clarity about the intent of the divine author—that is, God. This claim can be particularly insidious when it is used to dehumanize or otherwise do harm in the name of God. Holding on to dynamism and multiplicity in interpretation can mitigate against those kinds of totalizing interpretations.

oral traditions that fed their work. Then, having identified those authors, the idea is that we could somehow transport ourselves back into the authors' psyches and understand everything they had in mind as they produced the text. Furthermore, the question of intent also distills the meaning of a text to one "correct" or even "best" answer—like excavating the core nugget of meaning. To be sure, some readings are significantly better than others: better supported by textual evidence, more attentive to the ancient context, better undergirded by archaeological data, and so on. But the Bible is not a riddle to be solved or a code to be unlocked; we do not feed texts into hermeneutical computers and have them spit out a "right answer," and we certainly cannot put the authors on a psychiatrist's couch to analyze just what they were intending to say with their words. Although I will often refer to the "writers" or "authors" of the biblical text, those terms are mere ciphers for the complicated combination of oral tradition, writing, editing, discernment, and compilation that has brought the text in its current form to us today.

Complex Editorial History

The question of how biblical books were edited, or redacted, goes hand in hand with issues of authorship. Authorship and editing are both "diachronic" questions, analyzing the development of a text over time. (By contrast, questions of genre are predominantly literary and "synchronic," dealing with the final, received form of a text.) In our example of composite authorship from Numbers 22, we considered that the story of Balaam's talking donkey seems to be a remnant of a different tradition with a more negative appraisal of the character Balaam than that of the surrounding material in Numbers 22–24. We evaluated seams in the text from the perspective of identifying composite authorship—the joining together of two texts and/or traditions. Yet we also know that there was probably another hand at work in the text—namely, an editor who had the last say in stitching together the texts of the Pentateuch. Perhaps this happened at the same stage as joining the donkey story with the Balaam narrative, or perhaps it was later in the development of the book of Numbers or the Pentateuch as a whole. Regardless, the fact remains that others saw the composite nature of the text—including the donkey tale, clearly marked as an insertion with its resumptive repetition—and decided that preserving the text in all its dissonances was more valuable than smoothing out the narrative into a more cohesive presentation.[21]

Having just issued a word of caution about trying to pinpoint authorial intent as the end-all of interpretation, I share a similar caution about editorial intent. Of course, real human beings made these editorial decisions, and it is worthwhile to acknowledge that and to speculate about possible motivations. Were they interested in the preservation of traditions? Were they trying to develop a comprehensive national literature? Did they share a commitment to diverse voices? Were they simply bad editors who did not notice all the seams? Ultimately it is impossible to know the editors' rationale. We also do not know what other texts or traditions may have been cast aside or what other voices may have been deliberately silenced. Nonetheless, the overall effect of the editorial process has been to preserve dissonances in the text rather than to resolve or cover over them.

Dynamic Text, Dynamic Readers, Dynamic Spirit

Through much of this chapter we have dwelled on the dynamism of the Bible. Yet in our guiding metaphor of biblical interpretation as an atomic particle collision, we imagine both the text *and* the interpreter as atomic particles in motion, ready to collide.

---

21. For more examples of composite authorship, redaction, and the technique of resumption repetition, see Ska, *Introduction to Reading the Pentateuch*, 41–95.

Readers, too, are dynamic. Whether we realize it or not, each of us brings a particular set of assumptions and principles—a "hermeneutic"—to our interpretation of Scripture. That hermeneutic develops from an amalgam of our life experiences, our identities, and our theological influences, as well as any intentionally chosen paradigms or lenses through which we may be reading. We can try on new perspectives or work to set aside presumptions, but we will never read Scripture outside of our embodied, located selves.[22] Given that our experiences and even some elements of our identities will change over time, our interpretations will also shift. Indeed, no two encounters between a text and a reader—even the same text and the same reader—are ever quite the same.

Finally—or perhaps, primarily—I affirm the role of the Holy Spirit in interpretation. Different theological traditions within Christianity nuance the idea of the inspiration of Scripture in different ways. Nonetheless, a basic belief that is part of my own hermeneutic, and one I expect I share with many readers of this book, is that the Holy Spirit is present in the reading and interpreting of Scripture, not just in its composition and compilation. The Spirit is what energizes the "atoms" of both the reader and the text, making interpretation a generative, creative process. When it comes to reading for the future of the church, my hope is not to separate Spirit-filled readings and critical academic ones but instead to see them as part of the same process.

Rejecting the idea that there is one correct meaning or interpretation for any given biblical text expands the possibilities for newness in our understanding of God and God's relationship with humanity. It also mitigates against the abuse of power by those who might claim irrefutable clarity about the mind of God. At the same

---

22. William P. Brown notes, "Exegesis is all about becoming a better reader not only of the text in all its otherness but also of the reader's subjectivity in all its familiarity" (*Handbook to Old Testament Exegesis*, 11). For an excellent introduction to biblical interpretation with attention to the locatedness of readers, see Smith and Kim, *Toward Decentering the New Testament*, 11–30.

time, this embrace of multiplicity also raises the question of adjudication: What is to say one reading is better than another? How do we know which readings proceed from the Spirit and which are merely hot air? The insights of critical biblical scholarship are indeed helpful in this process, especially inasmuch as they push us to craft evidence-based arguments to support our interpretations. However, no approach to reading the Bible, be it biblical studies in an academic classroom or a Bible study in a church basement, frees us from an accompanying process of discernment, in which our theological dispositions, moral values, spiritual disciplines, life experiences, and intellectual instincts coalesce to help us decide which interpretations are worth picking up and which should be set down. Leaning into the Bible's inherent multiplicities does not cloud our interpretive vision any more than any other approach to reading Scripture. On the contrary, acknowledging the Bible's dynamic innovations will give us a more expansive, generous view of the possibilities and promise of biblical interpretation for the future of the church.

2

Adapting Popular Culture

> The Scriptures are exceedingly "respiratory": they breathe in the culture of their times, and breathe it back out in a different form.
>
> Christopher B. Hays, *Hidden Riches*, p. 4

In today's digital, commerce-driven world, content that qualifies as "popular culture" is easy to identify, if also vast and ever-changing. Metrics such as webpage views, Twitter followers, Facebook likes, YouTube channel hits, and sales data provide quantifiable indications of the books, songs, movies, videos, and memes that are most widely accessible and that are enjoyed by the most people.[1] Tracking what qualifies as popular culture in the ancient Near East is more difficult. Only a small percentage of ancient civilizations' material culture survives for scholars to

1. Definitions of popular culture are contested among cultural theorists. Here I follow Fred E. H. Schroeder's emphasis that "mass production, mass distribution and mass communication are the primary distinguishing features of popular culture" (*5000 Years of Popular Culture*, 8) and especially that such communication is mediated through political, religious, or economic structures, rather than the one-to-one transmissions that characterize both elite and folk culture.

analyze. Low literacy rates, combined with the expense of textual production, meant that written materials were usually in the
purview of ancient Near Eastern societies' elites, rather than the
populace at large. The songs, games, dramas, and jokes that were
surely part of everyday life in ancient Israel and shared by oral
tradition are largely lost to us now.

Despite these limitations, there are several genres of texts, as
well as literary motifs, that have surfaced repeatedly in the archaeological and textual records of ancient Israel and its surrounding
societies in ways that suggest these types of stories were widely
known and much beloved. Among these text-types are ancient
Near Eastern flood stories, such as Genesis 6–9, and court stories,
such as Genesis 37–50, Daniel 1–6, and the book of Esther. In
this chapter I will show how the biblical presentations of these
two genres—flood stories and court stories—take popular literary themes of their day and adapt them to make particular claims
about ancient Israel and its God. As I lay out the similarities and
differences across multiple versions of each genre, I hold this question at the heart of our exploration: *What hope does the existence
of these parallels offer for the life, work, and future of the church?*

Considering the Bible's relationship to ancient popular culture
does not require succumbing to the notion that church must be
"entertaining" above all else, nor is this a call simply to repro-
duce in our current era the methods of text formation we are
observing here. Rather, by thinking about these biblical texts in
relation to an ancient "popular culture," we are awakened to the
ways that the church, too, is already steeped in the culture(s) that
surrounds it. Does your congregation have a Facebook page? If
so, it has adapted a storytelling tool of today's popular culture to
make claims about its own identity. Similarly, the communities of
ancient Israel represented in the flood narratives and court tales
told their own stories in relationship to, and influenced by, the
world around them. Then, as now, new experiences and new circumstances generated new stories and new modes of storytelling,

always with ancient Israel's covenant relationship with God at their core. I am hopeful that the more attuned Christian leaders are to the intercultural give and take within the biblical texts, the better equipped our faith communities can be for creative and strategic innovation led by the Holy Spirit. As you read, I invite you to reflect on your own community's story: what it says, how it is told, what forms the core of its identity, and what could be changed to communicate that story for a new day.

Popular Culture in Ancient Israel

Much of today's popular culture is associated with entertainment: television, movies, music, books, and social media. Although the Bible does not necessarily jump to the forefront of our minds when we think about "fun" today, the Old Testament contains many texts that had entertainment value in the ancient world, including the ones we will study in this chapter. A story set in the divine realm might well have had religious implications, but those were not divorced from the fact that hearing the story was a pleasant diversion. In other words, many of the texts that we now consider sacred were simply the literature of the day. Though it seems an obvious point, it is important to remember that the ancient Israelite religion, whose practice is reflected in biblical texts, was not yet a religion "of the book"; the classification and canonization of the group of books we know as the Hebrew Bible came even later. Thus as we consider how these narratives *adapt* popular culture, we are also simply marking that they *were* popular culture. In their early days, they were not yet in a book set apart and revered in the way we might think of the Bible's authority today.

Given the low rates of literacy in the ancient world, a life surrounded by written texts was the experience of the scribal class, a small minority of the population who were rigorously educated. The contact most people would have had with texts outside of a scribal life was actually in oral form, read aloud or recited. The first and best audience for texts was the scribes themselves, a fact that might tempt us to change our label "popular culture" to "high culture," something that is in the purview of the elites. If we want to attempt any study of the storytelling culture of the ancient world, the literary record is largely what is left to us to analyze; there are, of course, no audio recordings of oral tradition from the first millennium BCE. At the same time, it is safe to assume that many of the stories that were written down over and over were ones known outside of the scribal schools: received by scribes to write down and read or told by scribes to their families and communities. Despite the absence of mass media in the ancient world, we can still be assured of these stories' general popularity.

The book of Proverbs is a helpful place to observe the crossover between the educational setting of the scribal tradition and the practical teachings of ordinary daily life. Proverbs, like Ecclesiastes and Job, is part of the Hebrew Bible's "wisdom literature," which comments on how to live a successful, righteous life.[2] Wisdom literature is a deeply "scribal" genre, associated with the profession throughout the ancient Near East and reflecting the breadth of the scribe's vocation as teacher and scholar. The sayings that constitute the book of Proverbs are attributed to kings, such as Solomon, king of Israel (Prov. 1:1; 10:1; 25:1), who had a reputation for being especially wise, and also to anonymous sages, dubbed simply "the wise" (22:17). Although many of the proverbs reflect the concerns of the rich and powerful, others are more universal in scope, using imagery drawn from family life and the natural world, and more reflective of folk wisdom: "Better is a dinner of vegetables where love is / than a fatted ox and hatred with it" (15:17). Scribes received and promulgated popular oral

2. Wisdom literature is another example of a biblical genre that is deeply influenced by parallel traditions in nearby cultures but is also infused with a uniquely Israelite theological claim—namely, that "the fear of the LORD is the beginning of wisdom" (Prov. 1:7). See Longman, "Proverbs."

sayings in written form, even as they were also transmitting texts among elites.

We know that the scribes behind the Bible were deeply engaged with the culture of their time. They were not set apart in some bubble of righteousness, removed from the rest of the world. To be sure, the center of many scribes' lives was the temple. Nonetheless, we should not conflate ancient scribal life with images of medieval monasticism. Ancient Israelite scribes had families, and their profession was, in fact, their job: they were paid for it, and it provided them with financial security. Many scribes worked for the king and/or the state, where they navigated or even steered national and international politics. However we may characterize the presence of God in the formation of the Bible, we must also reckon with the presence of the world in that formation.

To understand popular literary culture in ancient Israel, we must also think *across* the cultures of the ancient Near East. The genres I am considering "popular" here did not originate in Israel, nor were they confined to it. As we have already seen in chapter 1, ancient Near Eastern civilizations were by no means closed off from one another. Military incursions, famine, trade, fortune-seeking: all were conditions that facilitated the movement of people across borders. The Hebrew Bible's provisions for care of the stranger—a sojourner in the land—testify further to how plentiful the opportunities were for intercultural contact. With the movement of people came the sharing of old stories and the development of new ones; difference has always fueled innovation. Moreover, cross-cultural learning was a staple of the scribal experience in Israel and its surrounding civilizations alike. As Karel van der Toorn writes, "Scribes interpreted texts and tongues: the knowledge of foreign languages was part of their profession. The cosmopolitan spirit of scribal culture made it open to influences from the outside world."[3] While the Hebrew Bible tells the stories

---

3. Van der Toorn, *Scribal Culture and the Making of the Hebrew Bible*, 53.

of one particular people, those stories were birthed through—not despite—multicultural influences.

Ancient Near Eastern Creation and Flood Stories

When the days of rain that accompanied slow-moving Hurricane Florence caused catastrophic flooding in the Carolinas, multiple news stories described the storm as a disaster of "biblical proportions." Epic, destructive, cosmic, devastating: these are the kinds of adjectives associated with Old Testament tales in today's popular imagination and in particular with the flood story of Genesis 6–9. The flood is big, and it is terrible.

The story of the flood is familiar even to people who have just a passing awareness of the content of the Old Testament. Disgusted with the corruption of humanity, God decides to destroy the earth and all that is in it, with one exception: the family of earth's one righteous man, Noah. God lets Noah in on the plan, instructing him to build an ark, load it with animals, and prepare to stay in it with his family for a while. Forty days and forty nights of rain flood even the highest mountains on earth, and all living creatures outside the ark die. Noah, his family, and the animals in the ark survive to repopulate the earth once the waters have subsided.

As recognizable as this narrative is in the twenty-first century, chances are good that the basics of the plot would also have sounded familiar to the earliest audiences of Genesis 6–9. The biblical account is, according to overwhelming scholarly consensus, dependent on earlier Mesopotamian narratives. The strongest evidence for this dependency is the significant chronological distance between the earliest surviving editions of the Mesopotamian narratives and the composition of the biblical account. Stories about a great flood and a single human survivor were circulating in writing around the ancient Near East since at least 1700 BCE, and they likely existed in oral tradition well before that. By contrast, the biblical flood story as we know it today dates from around the sixth century BCE, and any written account of a flood from ancient Israelite tradition could not predate the tenth century BCE. In other words, the Mesopotamian stories are old; the biblical account is, by comparison, young. The regional climate is another source of evidence: the experience of unpredictable, significant, and even catastrophic flooding would have been well known in Mesopotamia, the "land between the rivers," where both the Tigris and the Euphrates regularly, and sometimes suddenly, overflow their banks. By contrast, the arid climate of Syria-Palestine makes such a deluge unheard of there, and therefore an unlikely source for the origins of such a story.[4]

A general assertion of dependency, however, does not mean that the details of that relationship are settled. Generations of readers have mapped out the parallels between these stories to consider a host of questions: Did the biblical writers look at the text of a Mesopotamian flood story or have one directly in mind when composing the account we know in the Bible? Does the biblical story more closely resemble one particular Mesopotamian account? What is the relationship between each flood account and its surrounding narrative context? How do the stories differ in their depictions of the divine and the human? Does one of the separate threads of the biblical story—sources referred to as "J" and "P"[5]—bear more resemblance to the Mesopotamian versions than the other?

In biblical scholarship, this approach of drawing connections across ancient cultures and mapping out parallel texts is called "comparative study." It is often the stuff of seminary classrooms, but it is rarely a lively topic in the everyday work of the church.

---

4. Day, "Comparative Ancient Near Eastern Study" (see esp. pp. 75–77). See also Dalley, *Myths from Mesopotamia*, 1–8. There are also more granular arguments for dependency, such as the borrowing of particular Akkadian words. See Day, "Comparative Ancient Near Eastern Study," 81–82.
    5. See the section "Source Criticism" in this chapter for an explanation of these separate threads.

Comparative study is sometimes utilized for polemical ends, particularly in the realm of apologetics. Some readers have used the comparisons and contrasts among flood stories to argue for the moral or literary superiority of the biblical tradition over its Babylonian counterparts, claiming that the differences between the stories point to a more advanced civilization and/or a "better" God. Other readers have also used the similarities to argue for the historical reliability of the Bible, claiming that all the stories are different renderings pointing to a single historical event. Still others have taken the same data to claim that since the Bible is neither a historical account nor altogether unique, it is therefore not spiritually authoritative or that its culturally dependent origins somehow mitigate against the existence of God.[6]

My goal here is not to argue for the literary merits of any one text over another, nor is it to measure the value of the theological claims within the stories themselves. Moreover, I will set aside questions of historicity, such as whether a big flood really happened and whether any parts of the Bible accurately reflect those circumstances. My questions are not historical; they are literary and pedagogical: *How does the Bible tell the flood story, and why does it matter?*

Atrahasis: *A Mesopotamian Story of Creation and Flood*

In the book of Genesis, the flood story follows closely behind the creation accounts in Genesis 1 and 2 as part of the overall Primeval History—stories of the earliest days of the world—found in Genesis 1–11. Like the biblical version, the flood story in *Atrahasis* also follows an account of the creation of humankind. The story opens at the time "when the gods instead of man / Did the

---

6. For a helpful overview of polemical interpretations across the history of comparative study, see Hays, *Hidden Riches*, 15–38.

work, bore the loads . . ." (I.i).[7] The Igigi, or lesser gods, have been made to do the most difficult labor, such as digging the earth's rivers, by the Anunnaki, the higher gods. The Igigi revolt against the Anunnaki, who eventually call for mortals to be created in order to relieve the Igigi and take on the work. The first human is created by mixing clay with the flesh and blood of a slaughtered god. With these details, *Atrahasis* already bears striking similarities to the early chapters of Genesis. In the creation story found in Genesis 2:4–25, "the LORD God formed man from the dust of the ground, and breathed into his nostrils the breath of life; and the man became a living being" (v. 7).[8] In both stories an element of the earth is animated with an element of the divine.

Work is also a shared theme in both portrayals of the primeval world. For *Atrahasis*, labor is irksome to all the gods, who pass the burden down the hierarchy of power from the greater deities to the lesser deities and then finally to humans. In the Genesis 2 account, God places the first human in the garden of Eden "to till it and keep it" (v. 15). Later, the hallmark of life for the man after eating the fruit of the forbidden tree is for the ground he works to be cursed: "In toil you shall eat of it all the days of your life" (3:17). The creation account in Genesis 1:1–2:3 puts a different spin on the theme of work, depicting God's creative work as labor, from which God then rests on the seventh day. This detail provides an etiology, or origin story, for sabbath laws (Gen. 2:2–3; cf. Exod. 20:8–11).

In the myth of *Atrahasis*, while the creation of humanity solves the problem of the gods' workload, it creates another: human beings are just too noisy. The more they multiply, the noisier they get. Their clamor disturbs Ellil, and he conspires with his fellow high gods, the Anunnaki, to reduce the human population. The gods make several attempts to thin the numbers of people on

---

7. All translations are from Dalley, *Myths from Mesopotamia.*
8. For more on the two creation stories of Genesis, see the section "Source Criticism" in this chapter.

earth, using drought, disease, and starvation. However, each attempt fails, thanks to the intervention of the god Enki through the human Atrahasis. In each case Enki tells Atrahasis, whose name means "very wise," to instruct the rest of humanity not to make any offerings to any god except the one who has sent the given plague, a strategy that then shames the deity into relenting. Take, for example, this passage, when the god Adad has withheld the rain, and drought has fallen on the land:

> They did not revere their god(s),
> Did not pray to their goddess,
> But searched out the door of Adad,
> Brought a baked (loaf) into his presence.
> The flour offering reached him;
> He was shamed by the presents
> And wiped away his 'hand'.
> He made mist form in the morning
> And in the night he stole out and made dew drop,
> Delivered (?) the field (of its produce) ninefold, like a thief.
> [The drought] left them,
> [The gods] went back [to their (regular) offerings]. (II.ii)[9]

The strategy of bringing offerings to Adad, the very god who has instigated the drought, shames him, and he immediately brings rain and dew, drawing out the crops from the previously parched fields.

After this cycle repeats itself several times, the greater gods decide that rather than thinning the population, they must destroy humanity completely. A great flood becomes their method of choice. This time Enki tells Atrahasis to build a boat and to keep aboard his family and many animals while the rain falls: "For seven days and seven nights / The torrent, storm and flood came

---

9. Brackets and parentheses are reproduced from Dalley's translation and indicate gaps and other uncertainties from the original clay tablets.

on" (III.iv). When the storm subsides, Atrahasis offers a sacrifice: a burnt offering, food for the gods. The sacrifice makes the gods realize how much they have missed these offerings from humanity, but they also become angry at Enki for breaking the gods' oath that no life should survive. At the conclusion of the tale, the gods decree that some women will not give birth and that others will have stillborn children. In the world of the story, this solves the gods' problem of human overpopulation; in the pre-scientific world of ancient Mesopotamia, Atrahasis provides another etiology, this one explaining why some women are childless and why some infants die.

The parallels between Atrahasis and the Noah story are striking.[10] In each tale a deity (or deities) decides to destroy humankind via flood. A deity reaches out to one human being and warns him of the coming deluge, instructing him to build a boat, put his family in it, and wait out the storm. When the rains have stopped, each of the men makes an offering to his god, which creates a "pleasing odor" (Gen. 8:21) for the deity—a common way to describe offerings in Mesopotamia but the only place that particular description is used in the Hebrew Bible. If there were just two or three details in common between the stories, we might write them off as coincidental products of universally shared mysteries about how the world and its inhabitants came into being and about the concerns of everyday human existence, such as birth, human relationships, work, suffering, and natural disasters. However, when taking the overlaps in the flood stories together with the parallels in the accompanying creation stories, coincidence gives way to dependence.

It turns out that the biblical writers were not the first to adapt Atrahasis to produce a new work. Atrahasis was also integrated

---

10. Detailed comparisons between Mesopotamian flood stories and the biblical account are widely available (see, for example, "Flood Stories: Gilgamesh XI and Genesis 6–9," in Hays, *Hidden Riches*, 75–95). I am particularly influenced in this section by Day, "Comparative Ancient Near Eastern Study."

into the *Epic of Gilgamesh*, another ancient Mesopotamian tale. *Gilgamesh* recounts the adventures of Gilgamesh, king of Uruk, who is two-thirds god and one-third human, and his friend and companion Enkidu. Enkidu, a wild man nursed by animals, is sent to the rapacious Gilgamesh by the gods in an effort to restrain the king. After an extended wrestling match, the two men become friends and set off on adventures together. Eventually one of their exploits angers the gods, who punish the pair by killing Enkidu with disease. Enkidu's death sends Gilgamesh into deep despair, and he begins to grieve not only Enkidu but also the inevitability of his own death. He sets out to find a man named Utnapishtim, who was famous for having been granted immortality by the gods after surviving a great flood.

Tablet XI of *Gilgamesh* contains the flood narrative that is parallel to both *Atrahasis* and Genesis. The tablet preserves a fuller version of the flood than any of the other existing fragments of *Atrahasis*, allowing us to observe additional parallels with the biblical account. Utnapishtim's boat comes to rest on a mountain, Mount Nimush, just as Noah's ark "came to rest on the mountains of Ararat" (Gen. 8:4). After seven days, Utnapishtim releases first a dove, then a swallow, and neither finds a place to rest. Finally, he releases a raven, which does not return. This scene with the birds has a close echo in Genesis 8:6–12, wherein Noah sends out a raven and then periodically a dove to see if the waters have subsided. Although the name of the flood hero is Utnapishtim throughout *Gilgamesh*, Utnapishtim is twice called "Atrahasis" in Tablet XI, further supporting the idea that the existing myth was imported into *Gilgamesh*.

As striking as the overlap between all these stories is, the differences between the Mesopotamian versions and their biblical counterparts are just as stark; herein lie the biblical version's innovations. First is the primary theological difference between the two cultures: in Mesopotamia there are many gods, whereas ancient Israel acknowledges only one God, Yahweh. The biblical flood is both begun and ended, directed and resolved, by the same God. Of course, this change introduces a theological problem: If there are no other gods with whom to contend, what causes the one God to send—and then relent of—the deluge? Is this God capricious too? The Mesopotamian pantheon exhibits a certain combativeness; the gods are driven by their whims and cravings, and the conflicts between them mirror conflicts on earth. The cause of the flood is essentially humanity's noisiness, which is annoying to the gods. By contrast, the biblical story "ethicizes" the flood, attributing it to the violence and wickedness of humanity.[11] God's decision to destroy life by flood receives justification from human sin. (Whether that explanation is theologically satisfying or not remains a question to be debated elsewhere!) Relatedly, the hero Atrahasis is set apart because his "ear was open (to) his god Enki" (I.vii), but it is righteousness that characterizes Noah, in contrast to the rest of "thoroughly evil" humankind (Gen. 6:5 CEB). Humans' behavior *toward each other* is a concern of God's, while the Mesopotamian gods in *Atrahasis* are worried largely about how humanity bothers the gods themselves.[12]

By inserting the singular God of Israel into stories that previously presumed a pantheon, the crafters of the biblical narrative draw attention to God's oneness. God suddenly performs the functions of multiple Mesopotamian gods and goddesses; the God of Israel has singular control over the creation, and the same God who annihilates humanity also saves it. This monotheistic turn also emphasizes a certain closeness between God and humankind. Rather than functioning as a labor force for the divine or as collateral damage from conflicts between the gods, humanity is portrayed as *mattering* to God, having God's full attention,

---

11. Day, "Comparative Ancient Near Eastern Study," 84–85.
12. Some of the gods in *Atrahasis* display isolated moments of compassion for humans. For example, the goddess Nintu weeps as she sees the washed-up bodies after the flood (III.iv). The grief of the mother goddess is even more dramatic in the parallel text in *Gilgamesh*. See Day, "Comparative Ancient Near Eastern Study," 85.

sometimes with positive results and other times—as at the onset of the deluge—with negative ones.

As the inclusion of the flood portion of *Atrahasis* in Tablet XI of *Gilgamesh* attests, reworking existing material "was a pervasive part of scribal culture in the ancient Near East."[13] In that way, even the act of repurposing popular culture is itself a reflection of the Bible's enmeshment in its surrounding culture. Genesis 6–9 conveys a message about the singular power of the God of Israel and about God's concern for the ethical conduct of humanity. The outlines of the story are similar to known narratives, but the points of difference draw attention to a distinctive identity for this community and its God. New ideas are couched in familiar frameworks. For churches, the biblical flood stories testify to a certain inevitability of cultural influence; every writer, every institution, every believer will be shaped by the culture that surrounds her. At the same time, the flood story's parallels can call us to be reflective and intentional about the ways our faith communities interact with the world around us—and particularly with the ways the surrounding culture tells the stories that form its identities.

Source Criticism

Even a cursory review of the biblical flood narrative must not overlook another peculiarity of its composition—namely, that it is clearly the product of multiple, separate Hebrew sources that have been woven together to produce one account. Many scholars refer to these sources as the "Priestly" (P) source and the "Yahwistic" (J) source. They are among the four sources (J, E, D, and P) that traditionally constitute the Documentary Hypothesis, the theory that the Pentateuch is actually the product of the joining together of four distinct source documents.[14] Details of the theory

---

13. Hays, *Hidden Riches*, 88.

14. For an engaging introduction to the documentary hypothesis, see Friedman, *Who Wrote the Bible?*

remain fiercely disputed by scholars. It is unlikely, for example, that each source was ever a complete and cohesive "document," and the order, dating, and number of the Pentateuch's constitutive layers continue to be debated.[15] Nevertheless, the notion that the books of the Pentateuch are composite texts, and that particular characteristics within its texts point to distinct editorial hands, is a broad consensus among academic biblical scholars.

The accounts of creation in Genesis 1–2 provide a useful illustration of key characteristics of the J and P sources. (For this brief introduction, we can set aside the Elohist [E] and Deuteronomic [D] sources, since J and P dominate both the creation and the flood narratives.) The Priestly creation story is found in Genesis 1:1–2:4a. In it, God takes six days to create the world, speaks it into being ("Let there be light" [1:3]), creates humans last, and then takes the seventh day to rest. The second creation story, which begins at 2:4b, belongs to the Yahwistic (J) strand. It envisions God creating the first human before the appearance of any crops, "on the day the Lord God made earth and sky" (2:4b CEB). Whereas Genesis 1 describes women and men being created together, Genesis 2 describes the creation of one human who is later used to make a second human, now differentiated as a woman. The two stories are distinct literary units and different in their content. Each can stand alone as a complete narrative, and each offers a different account about the creation of the world.

In addition to variations in their content, the two creation stories also differ in their literary stylings. The Priestly story uses the Hebrew word *Elohim* for God throughout, appearing in most English translations as "God." The Yahwistic story, on the other hand, consistently uses *Yahweh Elohim*, usually translated as "the Lord God." The depiction of God in each story is different too. While God is portrayed as more cosmic and distant in Genesis 1, presiding over creation by voice and grand command, Genesis 2

15. See Ska, *Introduction to Reading the Pentateuch*.

presents a more anthropomorphic, intimate vision of God. God forms the human from dirt, shaping rather than declaring, and then blows the divine breath directly into the human's nostrils. God uses trial and error to find the human's mate, creating animals before settling on a second human formed from the rib of the first (Gen. 2:18–23). Later, in the garden of Eden—also part of the Yahwistic account—God walks in the garden and enjoys the evening breeze (3:8).

While the two different creation stories sit side by side in Genesis 1 and 2, the flood stories have been woven together to create one narrative. Although the story as we have received it in Genesis 6–9 is fairly cohesive, some "seams," repetitions, or other indications of composite artistry can be detected. Perhaps the most striking is the discrepancy in the number of animals brought into the ark. The famous image of one pair of every kind of animal marching onto the ark "two by two" comes from the Priestly source, which says, "From the clean and unclean animals, from the birds and everything crawling on the ground, two of each, male and female, went into the ark with Noah, just as God commanded Noah" (Gen. 7:8–9 CEB). However, according to the Yahwistic source, reflected in the text of God's command just verses earlier, the numbers depend on whether the animals are classified as clean or unclean: "From every clean animal, take seven pairs, a male and his mate; and from every unclean animal, take one pair, a male and his mate; and from the birds in the sky as well, take seven pairs, male and female, so that their offspring will survive throughout the earth" (vv. 2–3 CEB). Contained within the same narrative are contradictory tallies of the ark's passengers, one of many examples of the story's composite artistry.[16]

The composite nature of the Pentateuch amplifies our sense of the Bible's multiplicity. If our understanding of biblical authority

---

16. For a side-by-side comparison of the J and P elements of the flood story with corresponding lines from *Gilgamesh*, see Hays, *Hidden Riches*, 91–92.

hinges on whether the flood story contains a complete, accurate, and unique account of a single historical deluge—written by Moses, no less—then the presence of multiple sources, just like the reliance on pre-existing Mesopotamian flood narratives, becomes a threat. If, however, our understanding of biblical authority can embrace the Bible's multiplicity, then the many pieces and dependencies reveal the fullness of Scripture's vibrancy. We know that some editor—perhaps the author we know as the "Priestly" source—honored both past tradition and popular culture by weaving together Israelite takes on an ancient Mesopotamian flood narrative. The result is an innovative story that welcomes newness and difference, even as it argues for the singularity and potency of the God of Israel.

Court Stories

The stories of Joseph (Gen. 37–50), Esther, and Daniel and his friends (Dan. 1–6) are some of the most beloved tales in the Hebrew Bible. They provide popular content for church musicals and Vacation Bible School lessons, in part because of their gripping plotlines, heroic protagonists, and triumphant resolutions. Some of the stories, particularly some of those in Daniel, make bold theological claims, while others, such as the Joseph material, make only passing mentions of the deity. The book of Esther never mentions God at all. The narratives are to some degree didactic, but they are also deeply entertaining; they were surely read and preserved not only because they were instructive to ancient faith communities but also because they are fun, compelling stories. Lawrence Wills's remark about the book of Daniel could easily be applied to the Esther and Joseph stories as well: "Before it became scripture, *Daniel* was popular culture."[17]

While each of these stories preserved in the Hebrew Bible can be described broadly as a "short story," they all share an even

---

17. Wills, *Jewish Novel in the Ancient World*, 38.

more specific genre designation: "court tale." In the Jewish court tales, the heroes find themselves in service at the court of a foreign king. In that position the heroes either prove themselves to have superior wisdom, skill, and piety over other courtiers or, in the face of an existential threat, use their wisdom, skill, and piety to save themselves or their people. The court tale flourished in the sixth through fourth centuries BCE, an era that corresponds with the Persian Empire's rule over much of the ancient Near East.[18] The profusion of court tales surviving from that time suggests the genre was indeed a popular one, at least among the scribes responsible for transmitting it.[19] Writing in general—and therefore scribal employment—surged during the Persian era, thanks especially to the sprawling bureaucracy that the empire produced. Literate officials from lands the Persians conquered were put to work in service of the victorious king, conducting his business and producing official records. Many scribes had a front-row seat to life in the foreign court.

In the biblical court tales, scribes and their work are portrayed as ubiquitous, important, and even heroic. In the opening chapter of the book of Daniel, the title character and his friends are described as Israelite elites conscripted into service at the Babylonian court in the wake of the fall of Jerusalem: "They were to be taught the literature and language of the Chaldeans [i.e., the Babylonians]" (Dan. 1:4b). In subsequent stories, the four exiles rise through the ranks of imperial administration, albeit sometimes

---

18. Wills, *Jew in the Court of the Foreign King*, 39–42.

19. Given the high value of scribes and their work represented in these stories, it is little wonder that the texts were popular among their ranks. It is more difficult to say to what degree these texts were popular beyond the scribal class. Although literacy rates gradually increased as time went on, access to scrolls remained difficult and expensive for an everyday reader. Still, stories surely continued to be shared orally, as untraceable as that phenomenon may be. It is also fair to speculate that, when accessible, stories about palace intrigue captured the imaginations of those outside the royal court as well; one just has to look at the perennial popularity of the King Arthur legends, HBO's *Game of Thrones*, or even the abundant news coverage of the British royal family to see a sampling of modern analogues.

under different governments. Shadrach, Meshach, and Abednego hold authority over Babylonian administrative affairs, and after they survive Nebuchadnezzar's fiery furnace, they are promoted even higher in the kingdom. Daniel is described as "third in the kingdom" after he reads the writing on Belshazzar's wall (5:29) and then as a governor over all the satraps of the Persian king Darius (6:1–3). These stories' protagonists begin their journeys as exiles in service of the foreign king and end up as prosperous, valued, and powerful figures in his kingdom. Similarly, Joseph enters Egypt as a slave but rises through the administrative ranks to oversee Pharaoh's storehouses, becoming second in command to Pharaoh over all of Egypt (Gen. 41:40).

While the protagonists of the book of Esther do not begin the story as scribes, they end up with the power to write in the king's name (Esther 8:7–8), exercising a scribal function. The book of Esther is also studded with references to royal edicts, and a significant point of the plot hinges on the work of scribes. When Mordecai overhears two eunuchs plotting to kill the king, he exposes the conspiracy, and the king survives (2:21–23). The text notes, "A report about the event was written in the royal record with the king present" (v. 23b CEB). Later, on a night the king cannot sleep, he has the royal records read to him, presumably for their soporific effect. In those notations he discovers Mordecai's good deed, and he puts in place plans to honor Mordecai, further incensing Haman. The daily work of the anonymous palace scribes implicitly becomes an act of heroism, helping to enable Mordecai's rise in the story.

In addition to their scribal or administrative settings, the biblical court stories are set outside of Israel, reflecting the Jewish Diaspora of the early Second Temple period. Unlike other postexilic texts such as Ezra-Nehemiah, which contemplates the new shape of the Jewish community in Judah after the return from exile, the court stories focus on life for Jews who remain outside of the land. Esther is set at the winter palace belonging to the king of Persia in Susa, in what is now Iran. The Daniel tales, whose settings span several kingships under both Babylonian and Persian rule, take place in the courts of those kings. Even the Joseph story, which is set hundreds of years before the exodus, let alone the exile, centers most of its action in Egypt. Older, oral elements of the Joseph tale were shaped into the larger narrative as late as the early post-exilic period (ca. late sixth or early fifth century BCE).[20]

Ahiqar: An Aramaic Precursor

Like the creation and flood stories, the court tale as we have come to know it through the biblical material has its origins in Mesopotamia, as attested by the story of Ahiqar. This tale was likely composed in Aramaic in the seventh century BCE, and versions were copied and translated for centuries in multiple languages, leading James Lindenberger to describe it as "one of the best-known and most widely disseminated tales in the ancient Mediterranean world."[21] In other words, it is indeed representative of ancient Near Eastern popular culture. In some versions, a collection of sayings or proverbs attributed to Ahiqar is appended to the end of the story, while in later recensions, those sayings are interpolated into the narrative itself. The presence of those sayings—"The Words of Ahiqar"—attests to the character's reputation for wisdom. At the heart of the tale, though, is a narrative about Ahiqar's perils and successes in the courts of Assyria and Egypt.

At the outset of the story, Ahiqar is employed as a scribe and sage in the court of the king of Assyria. He raises his nephew, Nadin, as his son to succeed him in his work, but Nadin betrays him by falsely accusing him of sedition. The king orders Ahiqar's execution, but the sage survives by appealing to his executioner, Nabusumiskun, whose life Ahiqar once saved. Nabusumiskun and

---

20. See Hays, *Hidden Riches*, 110.
21. Lindenberger, "Ahiqar," 479. Similarly, John Collins calls it "one of the best-known stories of the ancient Near East." Collins, *Daniel*, 41.

Ahiqar hatch a plan to hide Ahiqar and kill another man in his place. Later Pharaoh, the king of Egypt, demands Assyria send an architect who can assist him with constructing a castle between heaven and earth. If Assyria cannot meet this demand, they must pay a penalty worth three years' tribute. The king regrets having ordered Ahiqar's execution, as only his wisdom could have met Pharaoh's challenge. At this point Nabusumiskun admits to the ruse and presents Ahiqar, who is dispatched to Egypt by the king. In Egypt Ahiqar matches wits with Pharaoh, answering his riddles and returning to Assyria with three years of tribute *from* Egypt. He thus outwits the foreign king and achieves prosperity for his own land, in addition to having defended himself against his enemies at home.

Although the story of Ahiqar is attested in multiple cultures, it found a particularly receptive audience among Jews in the Second Temple period. An extant manuscript of the story in Aramaic was discovered at the Jewish military garrison in Elephantine, Egypt. The character Ahiqar also appears in the book of Tobit, canonical in Catholic and Orthodox traditions and part of the Protestant Apocrypha. Although Ahiqar does not take center stage in the book of Tobit, he is named as Tobit's nephew and intercedes for him with the Assyrian king Esar-haddon at the beginning of the story. Then, near the end of the book, Tobit refers to the well-known story of Ahiqar's betrayal by his nephew, there called Nadab, as a cautionary tale. Most remarkably, the court story genre, of which Ahiqar is the early exemplar, was taken up by early Jewish scribes and reshaped into multiple biblical texts we know today.

Functions of Court Stories

What was it about Ahiqar, and stories like his, that captured the imagination of Jewish scribes in the early post-exilic period?

As humorous and compelling as they are, the court tales seem to have struck a chord with their first readers beyond simply providing good entertainment. It is likely that scribes in Diaspora saw profound echoes of their own lives and challenges in these stories, regardless of whether those historical scribes were indeed conscripted into service at the king's court or were simply making their way as foreign exiles in Babylonian everyday life. Inasmuch as the Jewish court stories are a product of popular ancient Near Eastern culture, they are also windows into the struggles for identity and theological meaning that faced ancient Jews in Diaspora after the exile.

Whereas Ahiqar was an Assyrian sage serving in the Assyrian court, the Jewish court tales all depict the heroes serving in foreign contexts. This shift is one of the primary innovations the biblical tales make to this popular literary form; as Carol Newsom remarks, "They added ethnic and religious tensions to the professional tensions already present in the court tale genre."[22] Surviving in a new land required a significant degree of assimilation to the ruling culture. The protagonists of the Danielic tales are given new Babylonian names when they enter the service of the empire. Daniel becomes Belteshazzar, Hananiah becomes Shadrach, Mishael becomes Meshach, and Azariah becomes Abednego (Dan. 1:6–7). Joseph is renamed Zaphenath-paneah by Pharaoh when Pharaoh makes him second in command over Egypt (Gen. 41:45). Esther, too, is known by two names in the text: "Hadassah" is a Hebrew name, while "Esther" is of either Babylonian or Persian origin (Esther 2:7).

In addition to new names, the heroes undergo other transformations overseen by palace officials. Pharaoh gives Joseph new clothes and jewelry (Gen. 41:42). Esther is subjected to twelve months of cosmetic treatments (Esther 2:12). Daniel and his friends receive three years of indoctrination into Babylonian

22. Newsom, *Daniel: A Commentary*, 16.

thought (Dan. 1:4–5). Each of these transformations speaks to the significance of the cultural differences being navigated by each of these protagonists—and, no doubt, by the scribes who told their stories—as they move between their Israelite heritage and their new foreign imperial contexts. Each empire requires that they give up some part of their old selves to take on a new identity.

While the protagonists of all the biblical court tales share the experience of a bifurcation of their identity, their next steps vary across the narratives. Joseph and Esther use their new status as the kings' insiders to advocate for their families and their people, averting disasters of famine and genocide. Across the various stories in Daniel 1–6, Daniel and his friends draw "lines in the sand" in terms of their assimilation. They refuse to defile themselves by eating the palace rations (Dan. 1). Shadrach, Meshach, and Abednego refuse to worship the king's golden statue, and yet they will live (Dan. 3). Similarly, Daniel continues to pray to his God rather than the king, and yet he will survive a stint in a den of lions (Dan. 6). Daniel also interprets dreams and prospers, even as he prophesies against the foreign monarchs (Dan. 2; 4; 5). Across all the stories, the Israelite heroes flourish in their foreign courts under exceedingly dire circumstances.

How would these stories have sounded to their first hearers, including the scribes who promulgated them? Commentators have proposed several possible functions for the court tales in their original context. The first is about survival in empire, what W. Lee Humphreys has called a "lifestyle for diaspora."[23] In this reading, the stories provided examples of how Jews could survive and thrive outside of Israel and under foreign rule, while still maintaining a particular Jewish identity. The courtiers prosper *within* the existing power structures and even actively work to support them; they do not envision an overthrow of the ruling

---

23. Humphreys, "Lifestyle for Diaspora." Similarly, Wills has emphasized that the court tales "assert the wisdom and statecraft of the cultural hero of the ruled ethnic group" within a multiethnic context. Wills, *Jewish Novel in the Ancient World*, 68.

empire. The stories, in essence, show that their protagonists can "go along to get along" with the Gentile rulers, even while celebrating particular cultural distinctions, thus marking the stories as "accommodationist" literature.

Other readers, though, have identified the court tales as "resistance" literature.[24] Robert Williamson Jr. notes two types of resistance in the book of Esther: Mordecai's protest, wherein he refuses to bow down to Haman, and Esther's insider long-game, in which she "uses the men's underestimation of her to great advantage," saving her people from genocide.[25] Williamson notes, "In its original writing, and in its long liturgical use in the Jewish tradition, the book of Esther is a call to resistance against anti-Semitism and a celebration of the resilience of the Jewish people against all who would do them harm."[26] In his Daniel commentary, Daniel Smith-Christopher describes the book's protagonists as "openly hostile" to the foreign authorities and notes that the first six chapters contain "powerful images of lowly Jewish exiles standing with faith and courage before the very throne of the occupying (and militarily superior) emperor, overcoming his military and political power through the power of God."[27] While they may not call for the armed overthrow of the imperial regime—a scenario unlikely to be successful in any case—these texts push back against the wholesale co-optation of Jewish identity and practices in the face of imperial domination.

Resistance in the Joseph stories is harder to identify, since Joseph actively carries out the will of the empire, hoarding and controlling its resources and, at times, using his power in exploitative ways.[28] Nonetheless, when Joseph interprets Pharaoh's dreams,

24. For a detailed discussion of accommodation versus resistance in readings of Daniel, see Newsom, *Daniel: A Commentary*, 12–18.
25. Williamson, *Forgotten Books of the Bible*, 158.
26. Williamson, *Forgotten Books of the Bible*, 170.
27. Smith-Christopher, *NIB* 7:21.
28. See, for example, Genesis 42:6–17. For more on Joseph's imperial complicity, see Brueggemann, "Fourth-Generation Sell-Out," in *Inscribing the Text*.

he is also asserting God's power over Pharaoh; God is the agent not only of Pharaoh's dreams but also of the realities they foretell (Gen. 41:14–45). Newsom highlights similar theological claims in the Danielic tales, showing how they "contest the claims of power made by imperial rhetoric, asserting a counterclaim that ultimate sovereignty belongs only to the God of the Jews."[29]

Even the book of Esther, which contains no direct mention of the deity, still contains a cryptic affirmation of an ultimate triumph for the Jews, even if Esther refuses to intervene. Mordecai says to her, "Do not think that in the king's palace you will escape any more than all the other Jews. For if you keep silence at such a time as this, relief and deliverance will rise for the Jews from another quarter, but you and your father's family will perish. Who knows? Perhaps you have come to royal dignity for just such a time as this" (Esther 4:13–14). Implicit in these comments is a sense that the power of Persia is not ultimate and that the deadly edicts of the empire will not prevail, even if the empire itself stays in power.

For Newsom, the theological affirmations in the court stories do not qualify as "resistance," since they do not ultimately undermine implementation of the imperial structures. In fact, as she writes, "The *system* of Gentile imperial rule is ideologically stabilized by showing how it can be consistent with claiming the ultimate sovereignty of the God of the Jews."[30] At the same time, the stories do not fall in lockstep with all the whims of the conquering monarchs but instead push back against their totalizing power in all the ways described above. Of course, the functions of the court tales need not have been limited to any single possibility; readers take what they need from a story. Moreover, each of the tales is distinct from the others. The authors of these tales did not simply take a narrative formula and plug in new details. The scribes who crafted the Jewish court tales adapted the genre

---

29. Newsom, *Daniel: A Commentary*, 16.
30. Newsom, *Daniel: A Commentary*, 16.

to tell new stories for a new age. No longer did life as descendants of Abraham, Isaac, and Jacob center on the Promised Land. War, exile, and resettlement shifted Israel's storytelling lens away from Judah to foreign citadels like Susa and Babylon.

The court narratives are largely fictional; there is no evidence, for example, that there was ever a Jewish queen of Persia such as Esther, and it is exceedingly unlikely that a single human being—Daniel or anyone else—could have lived long enough to serve courts spanning the more than one hundred years between the reigns of Nebuchadnezzar and Darius. At the same time, each of these stories has the texture of a historical account and includes an accurate depiction of the period in which it is set, like any good historical novel or period movie. Think, for example, of how the TV show *Mad Men* captured the values and aesthetics of 1960s Madison Avenue, yet featured fictionalized characters at an invented advertising agency. In a similar way, the court tales offer a convincing window into post-exilic Diaspora life, but they communicate ideas that reach far beyond the confines of "history."

The content of the biblical court tales prompts our faith communities to consider vital questions of identity, piety, and belonging in the midst of a rapidly changing world. In what ways do we accommodate the powers of this world, and where must we resist them? How do we define our community and our religious practices, maintaining a unique identity and purpose that are over and against oppressive political forces? At the same time, the *form* of the biblical court tales—that is, of a popular genre repurposed for a particular community in a particular era—also prompts us to consider the ways in which we tell our stories, both within our communities and to the world at large. What might it mean to think beyond the church newsletter and the pulpit sermon? Are there poems or novels, letters or podcasts, tweets or photographs that would testify to your story in invigorating ways? Thinking expansively and creatively about storytelling will also mean identifying your community's core values and identities. What is your unchanging center, and where is there flexibility in how you communicate it?

Ancient Popular Culture and the Church

What are the foundational stories of your community? Who tells them, and how are they being told? The formation of the biblical flood story and court stories reminds us all that we do not form faith communities in a vacuum, devoid of any interaction with the world around us. On the contrary, our worship practices, religious spaces, social influence, membership, and mission—all parts of "doing church"—are affected by or are in conversation with the many overlapping cultures that we participate in and that surround us. These may include regional, national, ethnic, and economic cultures—as well as the "popular" culture that often crosses over those other categories. "Church," too, is its own kind of culture, with variations according to denomination, size, liturgical styles, etc. By tuning in to the ways our faith communities navigate complex cultural matrices, we may also become aware of the ways we have neglected vital aspects of our own identities or have neglected to "translate" our core commitments in ways our broader communities can understand and to which they can relate.

A word of caution is in order: this call to consider how we may learn from the Bible's adaptation of ancient popular culture is decidedly *not* a call for the imperializing practice of "cultural appropriation," the wholesale co-optation of the forms or practices of another—especially minoritized—culture for the benefit of a dominant culture. Rather, it is a call for reflection and awareness of the ways this broad category of "culture" is part of church life and a call to engage it responsibly, with a willingness to listen and to learn. In other words, the church is steeped in the world; it does not exist apart from it. This "worldliness" is as old as the Bible itself, and it is a fact to be embraced, not hidden or denied.

The biblical account of the great flood argues for ancient Israel's particular vision of Israel and its God—namely, the oneness of God and God's sustained attention to humanity. The story uses variations on an existing popular genre to communicate that vision. The fact that multiple sources have been woven together to make the whole testifies to the multiplicity baked into the Bible's very pages. At the core of the flood story is the oneness of God; the means of communicating that oneness are many and varied, not only within the flood narrative but also across the Old Testament as a whole. That multiplicity offers hope: there is neither one right answer to the question of how to live out the faith nor one superior way to tell the stories of our communities and our God. Instead, the Bible witnesses to deep engagement with the world and its many and varied storytelling tools.

Perhaps more than any other part of the Old Testament, each of the court stories reflects specific concerns of the scribal class, with good reason: they were post-exilic Israel's public storytellers. They had the means and the opportunity not only to write down earlier oral traditions but also to compose new written texts for a new era. They drew on a popular literary form of their day—one known not only in ancient Israelite circles but also in the broader ancient Near Eastern world—to give voice to their experience of displacement, crafting tales of hardship and triumph full of humor and promise. Thus the stories reflect both a broadly popular culture form and the particularities of scribal culture. Whether the genre functioned as survival guide or religious testimony, source of spiritual inspiration or blueprint for resistance, the stories provided hope for a community in turmoil.

Reflecting on the scribal authorship of the court stories should also prompt us to ask, *Whose stories are* not *told here?* Of course, all stories are situated in a particular place and time, and these scribal tales provide both a valid and a vital window into post-exilic life. Nevertheless, as tales of Diaspora, they do not necessarily reflect the concerns of those who returned from exile to Judah or, especially, of those who never left. As 2 Kings 25:12 recounts, "The captain of the guard left some of the poorest people of the land to be vinedressers and tillers of the soil." Whereas Ezra-Nehemiah voices the interests of many of the returnees (albeit not in the same "popular" storytelling format), no biblical text clearly reflects the perspectives of those who remained in the land.

Likewise, we must ask in and of our own faith communities, Whose stories are not being told? Whose stories are highlighted in our narratives, and whose are neglected? How has our community's story changed over time? Would trying new *forms* of storytelling amplify different voices and better communicate our stories for a new era? Innovation has many dimensions. The flood story and court story alert us to the possibilities for adopting new modes of storytelling as the world changes and as the church changes with it. In the next chapter, we will see that the Bible also showcases fundamental theological innovations within the biblical timeline.

3

Rethinking Theological Assumptions

In chapter 2 we looked at examples of the ways ancient Israel told its stories by reworking existing popular genres to make particular claims about the God of Israel. In this chapter we will observe that some of the claims and counterclaims we see in ancient Israel's literary output are not confined to cross-cultural dissonances but also reflect shifts within the Israelite tradition itself. I will highlight two moments in the history of Israel, as testified to in the Hebrew Bible, when some voices in Israel rethought particular elements of the ways they understood God to be encountered in community. The first theological innovation, the Deuteronomic centralization of worship in the late seventh century BCE, was born out of political expediency. The second innovation, Ezekiel's understanding of a shift in God's presence from the temple to among the exiles in Babylon, was spurred on by the communal trauma of the Babylonian exile. Each of these examples showcases the diversity within ancient Israelite theo-politics as well as how particular ideas changed over time in response to shifting circumstances. Rather than smoothing over changes, the Old Testament preserves them, providing us an extraordinary look at ancient theology in motion.

Rethinking Worship

According to 2 Kings 22, the high priest Hilkiah, on an administrative errand to oversee repairs to the Jerusalem temple in 622 BCE, finds "the book of the law in the house of the LORD" (v. 8). Hilkiah turns the book over to Shaphan, King Josiah's secretary, who then reads the book aloud to the king. The words of this book so startle Josiah that he consults Huldah the prophetess, who brings word from God that Israel is on its way to disaster because it has ignored the laws of the book. In response, Josiah gathers the people for a reading of the law and a renewal of their commitment to the covenant, which is later followed by a program of sweeping religious reforms. As told in 2 Kings 23, Josiah purges Jerusalem and Judah at large of any religious trappings that imply worship of a god other than Yahweh. He tears down the high places and sacred poles devoted to other gods, and he destroys their idols and libation vessels. He destroys Yahwistic sanctuaries outside of Jerusalem, and he even kills the priests presiding at sanctuaries in Samaria. He also oversees the celebration of the Passover as prescribed in Deuteronomy—that is, observed by pilgrimage to the central sanctuary (Deut. 16:1–8) rather than by each household slaughtering an animal at home (Exod. 12:1–13).

The program of reform described in 2 Kings 22–23 is consistent with the theological outlook of the book of Deuteronomy, which emphasizes worship at a central sanctuary and covenant fidelity to Yahweh. In fact, since Wilhelm de Wette first proposed the idea in 1805, many scholars have understood the book unearthed in the temple to be some form of Deuteronomy, such as chapters 12–26, which are its legal core. Along with that proposal come questions about the relationship of the book of Deuteronomy as we know it to this found book in the story of Josiah. Is it, as the biblical text narrates, an older scroll forgotten in the dusty archives of the temple and then finally implemented to full effect under the pious reign of Josiah? Is it, as many scholars now hold, that the heart of Deuteronomy was not rediscovered from the past but rather was created during the reign of Josiah in the seventh century BCE to support his political agenda? Or is it, as still others claim, a directive more reflective of Second Temple worship from the fifth century BCE than of the pre-exilic era?[1]

Despite the debates over the dating of Deuteronomy's composition, scholars generally agree that the centralization of worship called for in the book of Deuteronomy and in Josiah's reforms reflects an innovation in ancient Israelite worship practices introduced in 622 BCE or later. Regardless of whether this was a hoped-for ideal or an actual implementation, the idea that one would bring a sacrifice only to the Jerusalem temple rather than to a local shrine is a different outlook on worship than what is offered in other parts of the Pentateuch. The Covenant Code—widely regarded as a pre-exilic text—provides strong evidence for this difference.[2] Exodus 20:24 reads, "You need make for me only an altar of earth and sacrifice on it your burnt offerings and your offerings of well-being, your sheep and your oxen; in every place where I cause my name to be remembered I will come to you and bless you." Notice the implicit affirmation of multiple sanctuaries—"*every* place where I cause my name to be remembered."

---

1. For an excellent, accessible recap of the history of scholarship on the Deuteronomistic History, see Römer, *So-Called Deuteronomistic History*. Bernard M. Levinson sums up the dominant hypothesis, which I also share: "The narrative core of 2 Kings 22–23 is the work of a preexilic editor who sought to legitimate the introduction of a new set of laws and to sanction Josiah's cultic and political initiatives. That narrative was most likely supplemented in the exilic and postexilic periods." Levinson, *Deuteronomy and the Hermeneutics of Legal Innovation*, 10.

2. The "Covenant Code" refers to the legislative texts in Exodus 20:22–23:33. It is one of the three major groupings, or "codes," of laws in the Pentateuch. The others are the Deuteronomic Code (Deut. 12:1–26:15) and the Holiness Code (Lev. 17–26), though some scholars prefer to designate all of Leviticus 1–26 as the Priestly Code.

Contrast this with Deuteronomy 12:10–11: "When you cross over the Jordan and live in the land that the LORD your God is allotting to you, and when he gives you rest from your enemies all around so that you live in safety, then you shall bring everything that I command you to the place that the LORD your God will choose as a dwelling for his name: your burnt offerings and your sacrifices, your tithes and your donations, and all your choice votive gifts that you vow to the LORD." The same passage goes on clearly to prohibit sacrifices at multiple sanctuaries: "Take care that you do not offer your burnt offerings at any place you happen to see. But only at the place that the LORD will choose in one of your tribes—there you shall offer your burnt offerings and there you shall do everything I command you" (12:13–14). The language repeated throughout Deuteronomy—"the place the LORD will choose," sometimes adding "as a dwelling for his name"—points to the central sanctuary in Jerusalem. The temple is not named explicitly, given that, according to the narrative's timeline, it has not yet been built. Yet by retrojecting that idea into the mouth of Moses at Horeb, the text harnesses ancient authority for a later idea.

Centralization of worship introduced a few practical quandaries for everyday Israelite life: how and when to eat meat, for example. In the Covenant Code, every slaughter of a domestic animal for meat required that the animal be killed on an altar and that part of the animal be offered as a sacrifice to God. In other words, Israelite worship prohibited what is often referred to as "profane slaughter"—or, to use a somewhat less fraught term, "secular slaughter." When an Israelite could take an animal to the local sanctuary, that prohibition was not a problem. Moreover, the Exodus text says that God will meet the worshipers where they are, whereas in Deuteronomy the worshiper is the one who must go to God—namely, to the central sanctuary, the one place (in Deuteronomic thought) that God chooses as a dwelling for his name. If every opportunity to eat meat required a pilgrimage to Jerusalem, then it potentially became a once-in-a-lifetime experience, rather than a regular (albeit still relatively infrequent) occurrence.[3] Deuteronomy addresses this issue by specifically allowing secular slaughter, even as it emphasizes that no sacrifices should be offered anywhere besides the Jerusalem temple: "Yet whenever you desire you may slaughter and eat meat within any of your towns, according to the blessing that the LORD your God has given you; the unclean and the clean may eat of it, as they would of gazelle or deer" (Deut. 12:15).

Bernard M. Levinson has shown that Deuteronomy 12 exegetically reworks Exodus 20:24 by echoing and carefully reusing its language, not only to assert the practice of centralization but also to draw on the authority of the older law and, by doing so, to supplant it.[4] Levinson emphasizes that centralized worship, along with its supporting transformations of animal slaughter, festival observances, and judicial procedures, represents a genuine and profound innovation in both the life of ancient Israel and its literary history. Levinson's meticulous work shows the careful scribal process of interpretation that went into the presentation of Deuteronomy. His book is emphatic in its descriptions of the dramatic and far-reaching way that Deuteronomy represents innovation: "The authors of Deuteronomy radically transformed the religion and society of ancient Judah. The innovation of cultic centralization profoundly changed sacrificial procedure, the festival calendar, judicial procedure, and public administration, including the monarchy. The new vision was as much political as it was religious. It led to a massive relocation of power, both centrally and locally."[5] This idea of laying out a religious belief and then exhorting people to follow it with practice is a bit backward from the usual understanding of ancient religion; we would

---

3. Oded Borowski notes that meat was not eaten every day in part because of the economic calculations involved, as animal husbandry was an investment for the herder. Borowski, *Every Living Thing*, 57–58.

4. Levinson, *Deuteronomy and the Hermeneutics of Legal Innovation*, 23–52.

5. Levinson, *Deuteronomy and the Hermeneutics of Legal Innovation*, 144.

expect the articulation of a belief or justification for it to follow an existing practice.[6] What may appear at first as a relatively benign, even banal process of literary redaction is shown by biblical scholarship to be a dramatic reorientation to tradition that had direct bearing on the everyday lives of ancient Israelites, even as it has also shaped the received text and the interpretation of it in the centuries since.

Patrick D. Miller's endorsement on the back of Levinson's book captures some of the import of these proposals for our current study: "Levinson's work is a clarification of the way in which hermeneutics is not something that starts with the interpreter's handling of the canonical text but is *a process by which the canonical text itself came into being*."[7] In other words, centralization of worship is evidence of the Bible's inherent, baked-in interpretive dynamism. Biblical texts are not blank slates when we interpret; the texts themselves are already interpretations, and readers are participants in that act. The innovations of Deuteronomy are especially remarkable because we can see the texts from which they proceed. Preserved for us in the canonical text of the Pentateuch are both older *and* newer, localized *and* centralized, striking a dissonant chord together, even as they are both offered as the voice of God through Moses. Innovation here is an accretion, not a replacement.

Why would the scribes in Deuteronomistic circles be rethinking the location of sacrificial worship in ancient Israel? The text does not leave us many clues. As with any written text, it is difficult if not impossible to assess the motivations of its authors, particularly when they are long dead. One possibility is simply that they were scribal allies of Josiah, and so they reworked tradition to

---

6. Cf. Meyers, "Women's Religious Life in Ancient Israel," 354: "Although their religious activities were shaped by their beliefs, religion was what people *did* rather than what they believed."

7. Patrick D. Miller, back cover of Levinson, *Deuteronomy and the Hermeneutics of Legal Innovation* (emphasis added).

provide "ancient" authority for his political strategy, which may simply have been to consolidate his power for the sake of power.[8] We can at least affirm that the Deuteronomic authors' theological reforms were surely driven by some theo-political agenda, even if the exact details of those motivations are lost to us now. Were they doing the "right thing" by advocating for centralization? Did they have holy or selfish motivations at heart? We should note that simply having an agenda is not in and of itself a disqualification from righteousness. Indeed, working to prove something or argue for something or advocate for something is something every reader does in her interpretation, whether intentionally or not. Nevertheless, I want to reiterate that I am not calling for anyone uncritically to replicate the innovations highlighted here. Instead, by tracing the lines of theological innovation revealed by biblical scholarship on the Old Testament, we are alerted to the Bible's many inherent multiplicities and the broadness of its thought, making us better equipped to discern for our own contexts what constitutes biblically informed innovation.

Rethinking the Location of God's Glory

It seems that most introductions to Ezekiel must begin with some acknowledgment of just how utterly strange the book is, and so I will add my voice to that chorus: Ezekiel is *weird*. The prophet reports many strange and alarming visions of wheels and domes, monsters and bones. He performs odd symbolic acts, such as swallowing a scroll and cutting and then variously manipulating sections of his hair. He also offers extended diatribes about Israel's

---

8. While some scholars have claimed that Josiah had a quasi-imperial strategy for taking the northern kingdom of Israel and re-creating a united kingdom, such theories assume far more coherence of the Davidic kingdom than likely existed. I find it more likely that Josiah's reforms were driven by anxiety about foreign invasion than by dreams of imperial grandeur. See also the critique of expansionist proposals in Kim, *Decolonizing Josiah*.

infidelity to Yahweh, using graphic imagery of sexual violence against women as a vulgar, violent metaphor for Israel's judgment. There are many reasons some readers—including me—generally keep their distance from Ezekiel. Despite the odd and sometimes downright disturbing imagery that dominates the book, Ezekiel's theological innovations broke new ground for their day. David L. Petersen has called Ezekiel one of "the most creative theological thinkers of all Israel's prophets," given Ezekiel's affinity for "taking a motif or element of tradition and pursuing it to a logical and theological conclusion."[9] Ezekiel's prophetic career is defined by two major features: his priestly interests and his experiences of the Babylonian domination of Judah, including exile. Having been deported to Babylon with the first wave of deportees in 597 BCE, he watches the coming fall of Jerusalem to Babylon from afar. He reckons with the loss of Jerusalem through the lens of priestly concerns, such as the temple, holiness, and, of particular interest for our study, the glory of God. In its engagement with the motif of God's glory, the book of Ezekiel tackles one of life's most enduring theological questions: In times of profound disaster, *where can God be found*?

Priestly Themes

Ezekiel is a prophet, in that he communicates visions and words from the deity, but he is also a Zadokite priest, trained in the theology and liturgics of the Jerusalem temple in the monarchic era. The Zadokites claimed a lineage from Zadok, a priest during David's reign who became the sole caretaker of the ark of the covenant after Solomon banished Zadok's colleague Abiathar for supporting Adonijah's claim to the throne (1 Kings 1–2). Ezekiel consistently asserts that the Zadokites are the only priests who should preside at the altar (e.g., Ezek. 44:9–16).[10] While it is diffi-

9. Petersen, *Prophetic Literature*, 158–59.
10. Ramsey, "Zadok."

cult to say whether Ezekiel ever had the opportunity to preside as a priest in the temple, given that his prophetic career commences in exile, he certainly espouses a priestly worldview. Broadly speaking, a priestly worldview includes an interest in the encounter with God via sacrificial worship and all concomitant issues, including ritual purity, liturgical stylings, and the temple as the dwelling place for God. For Ezekiel, the priestly themes I highlight below converge into a theological reassessment of holy space and access to the presence of God for a people in exile.

Zion Theology

For the Zadokite priesthood in the late monarchic era of ancient Israel, priestly theology emphasized the sacredness of Zion, the holy mountain chosen by Yahweh as his dwelling, as well as the chosenness of the Davidic lineage to rule in the holy city. The Zion tradition is exemplified in a handful of psalms as well as in several passages across the book of Isaiah.[11] Psalm 46 illustrates this tradition well. This psalm is especially familiar for its line, "Be still, and know that I am God" (v. 10a), as well as for being the inspiration for Martin Luther's hymn "A Mighty Fortress Is Our God." Arguably, though, it is the poetic description of the city of God and God's dwelling within it that constitutes the theological heart of the psalm:

> There is a river whose streams make glad the city of God,
>   the holy habitation of the Most High.
> God is in the midst of the city; it shall not be moved;[12]
> God will help it when the morning dawns.

11. Zion psalms include Psalms 2; 46; 48; 65; 76; 84; 87; 95–99; 110; 122; 125; 128; and 132. For examples of the Zion tradition in Isaiah, see Isaiah 26:1–7 and 60–62. For a more comprehensive list of Zion passages in Isaiah, see Levenson, "Zion Traditions."

12. The NRSV here clarifies that "God is in the midst of *the city*," whereas the Hebrew has only the third-person feminine pronoun, for which "city," a grammatically feminine noun, is the antecedent. In its formal and archaic way, the KJV renders these references to "city" with a feminine pronoun: "God is in the midst of her; she

> The nations are in an uproar, the kingdoms totter;
> 　　he utters his voice, the earth melts.
> The LORD of hosts is with us;
> 　　the God of Jacob is our refuge. (46:4–7)

Notice how steady and solid the city is, thanks to God's presence in the middle of it. It is well watered and deeply rooted, while realms around it are unsteady, fragile: "the kingdoms totter." Help is readily available because Zion is the dwelling place of God, God's "holy habitation."

Psalm 84 expresses Zion theology in the form of a hymn for pilgrims going to Jerusalem, focusing on the temple as the house of God. As the psalmist travels to the temple, he expresses a deep longing to be near God:

> How lovely is your dwelling place,
> 　　O LORD of hosts!
> My soul longs, indeed it faints
> 　　for the courts of the LORD;
> my heart and my flesh sing for joy
> 　　to the living God. (84:1–2)

The psalm goes on to affirm further that "the God of gods will be seen in Zion" (v. 7b). Like Psalm 46, Psalm 84 underscores that anyone who wants to find God knows where to look: in God's dwelling, the temple. Psalm 84 also adds an affirmation of the Davidic king, referred to as God's anointed:

> Behold our shield, O God;
> 　　look on the face of your anointed.
>
> For a day in your courts is better
> 　　than a thousand elsewhere.

---

shall not be moved." Despite the many memes that imply this verse refers to a human woman, God here dwells within the city—that is, Zion.

> I would rather be a doorkeeper in the house of my God
> than live in the tents of wickedness.
> For the LORD God is a sun and shield;
> he bestows favor and honor. (vv. 9–11)

Both God and the king are referred to in this psalm with the metaphor of a shield, further uniting the theology of Zion with God's divine favor of the monarch in Jerusalem. Other psalms even more overtly showcase the combination of the chosenness of Zion with the election of God's king. Psalm 2 depicts God striking terror into the hearts of other kings by telling them, "I have set my king on Zion, my holy hill" (v. 6). Then the king himself begins to speak, saying, "I will tell of the decree of the LORD: He said to me, 'You are my son; today I have begotten you'" (v. 7). As these brief examples illustrate, Zion theology is deeply rooted in a sense of place—that is, the temple on God's holy mountain in Jerusalem, where God sits enthroned. It also affirms the sovereign power of God over other peoples, and it emphasizes the chosenness of the Davidic king, who, in parallel to God's power but also dependent on it, also rules from his throne in Jerusalem.

Priestly Thought in the Pentateuch

"Priestly" is also a significant category in the study of the Pentateuch, where it takes on somewhat different resonances than in Zion theology. The "Priestly" source (P) is an authorial (or editorial) voice characterized by a particular vocabulary and set of concerns. We have already seen P at work in the creation story of Genesis 1, which emphasizes the cosmic dimensions of God's creative work and revels in the orderly separation and categorization of darkness and light, the waters above and the waters below, etc. We have also seen P interwoven with the J (Yahwistic) source in the flood narrative, where it shares a similar sense of cosmology and orderliness with Genesis.[13] P is associated with the specifications in Exodus of the tabernacle—God's traveling tent shrine that foreshadows the temple—as well as the sacrificial and purity regulations of Leviticus 1–16 and much of the book of Numbers.

The Priestly source's presence in the book of Exodus is of particular interest for our study of Ezekiel. When we think of Exodus, many of us probably think of the exodus *event*, the centerpiece of the dramatic first half of the book. Most readers are well acquainted with those first nineteen chapters, which detail the Hebrews' enslavement in Egypt, the call of Moses, the ten plagues, the escape through the parted sea, and the commencement of the wilderness wanderings. Much of the middle portion of the book, too, feels familiar, with the giving of the law at Sinai and the ratification of the covenant. The reader's attention is more strained, though, in chapters 25–31, when Moses is up on the mountain receiving the detailed instructions for the construction and furnishing of the tent of meeting. After all the action that precedes this section, the pure narrative drama seems to screech to a halt. In some ways this section feels as dry as Ezekiel feels odd. And yet the meticulous attention to detail bespeaks an interest in and dedication to *holy space*. The sheer number of column inches devoted to the sanctuary already signals how vital the tabernacle is in P's authorial worldview.

Exodus 32–34 provides a fast-paced interlude detailing the golden calf apostasy and its aftermath. Then attention returns to the tent of meeting for the final chapters of the book, wherein Moses and the people implement the instructions supplied in chapters 25–31. The construction comes to a climax in chapter 40, when, after Moses sets up the ark of the covenant inside the tabernacle, God enters it to dwell with Israel:

---

13. See under the heading "Source Criticism" in chap. 2. Cf. Ska, *Introduction to Reading the Pentateuch*, 60–65.

Then the cloud covered the tent of meeting, and the glory of the LORD filled the tabernacle. Moses was not able to enter the tent of meeting because the cloud settled upon it, and the glory of the LORD filled the tabernacle. Whenever the cloud was taken up from the tabernacle, the Israelites would set out on each stage of their journey; but if the cloud was not taken up, then they did not set out until the day that it was taken up. For the cloud of the LORD was on the tabernacle by day, and fire was in the cloud by night, before the eyes of all the house of Israel at each stage of their journey. (40:34–38)

Here the presence of God is represented by the "glory of the LORD." God's presence as "glory" is a recurring theme throughout the Priestly elements of the Pentateuch. For example, in Exodus 24:1–18, as Moses ascends Mount Sinai to receive the instructions for the tent and tabernacle, God's glory has settled on the mountain: "The glory of the LORD settled on Mount Sinai, and the cloud covered it for six days; on the seventh day he called to Moses out of the cloud. Now the appearance of the glory of the LORD was like a devouring fire on the top of the mountain in the sight of the people of Israel" (vv. 16–17). Cloud and fire characterize the glory: hazy and powerful—highly visible, yet not a sharply delineated form. When the tabernacle is complete, the glory is able to move from the mountain into the tent-shrine and to travel with the Israelites on the rest of their journey.

Most scholars now date the Priestly source to the exilic or early post-exilic period—contemporaneous with, or even after, the career of Ezekiel. Thus the detailed descriptions of the tabernacle are likely memories of the Jerusalem temple overlaid on the past. At the same time, the notion that a deity would dwell in a tent like the one described in Exodus has roots predating not only the book of Exodus but also the presumed date of the exodus event itself. In the literature from Ugarit, a Canaanite city-state that flourished in the middle of the second millennium BCE, the high god El lives in a tent. The tabernacle passages draw on ancient motifs even as they contemplate exilic theological questions. Jean-Louis Ska summarizes the post-exilic priestly theology this way, highlighting key vocabulary from P in quotation marks: "For the Priestly Writer, 'Israel,' which has been deprived of its political independence and monarchs, becomes a religious 'assembly' united around the divine presence, the 'glory.' 'Holiness,' a quality that defines places and individuals maintaining a privileged relationship with the divine presence (the 'glory'), is bestowed on the priesthood, tent, and altar (Exod. 29:44)."[14] The concerns about holy space, the glory of God, and where and how the people might encounter God are all interests shared by Ezekiel as he, too, contemplates what divine election and Yahwistic worship look like in what is, for the priests of ancient Israel, a dramatically changed world.

Before turning to the text of Ezekiel itself, we should attend to one more element of priestly thought in the Pentateuch: the Holiness Code, which appears in Leviticus 17–26. The Holiness Code is understood by many scholars to be the work of yet another Pentateuchal source because of the way it extends the holiness of the priests and the altar to the land of Israel and all its people. The Holiness source is part of a generally priestly worldview, but it is more like "Priestly source plus" or "P 2.0"; it is itself an innovation on P's regulations and perhaps even on Deuteronomic (D) ones.[15] Its orienting idea is found in Leviticus 19:2b, "You shall be holy, for I the LORD your God am holy." We saw above that the Covenant Code forbids secular slaughter but permits worship at multiple sanctuaries. Deuteronomy innovates on those regulations by permitting sacrifice only at the central sanctuary but allowing secular slaughter. The Holiness Code takes the stricter option from each code, permitting only sacrificial slaughter at the central sanctuary. The laws in the Holiness Code reflect both cultic

14. Ska, *Introduction to Reading the Pentateuch*, 190.
15. Ska, *Introduction to Reading the Pentateuch*, 151–53.

regulations and ethical ones; all the conduct of the community, whether cultic or ethical, can affect the purity of the sanctuary and of the land. Failure to follow the law can impede the community's encounter with God. Stephen L. Cook regards the Holiness strand, found in both the Holiness Code in Leviticus and in several other places scattered throughout the Pentateuch, as the most direct theological parallel to Ezekiel's thought and more or less synonymous with Zadokite theology.[16] If "priestly themes" were a Venn diagram, the area where the circles of Zion theology and Pentateuchal priestly thought overlap would be the Holiness strand. Dating the P and H sources, as well as laying out the layers of influence within the Bible's cultic tradition history, is a complex and contested issue, and a full outline of those questions is beyond the scope of our work here. Regarding the Pentateuch's priestly texts, we will simply note the thematic overlap; as John Kutsko puts it, "Ezekiel and P are . . . dipping into the same well of tradition."[17] However, when it comes to the influence of Zion theology on Ezekiel, we can more safely assume a chronological order: Zion theology precedes Ezekiel's reassessment of it in exile and is a paradigm from which he innovates.

Ezekiel and God's Mobility

We have taken this brief jaunt through various priestly ideas in the Hebrew Bible in order to get a broad sense of how Ezekiel's priestly identity would have elevated particular concerns for him, including the holiness of the temple, the temple in Zion as the dwelling of God, and God's covenantal relationship with the people. In the book of Ezekiel we encounter the collision of this priestly worldview with the reality of exile. Ezekiel prophesies from exile in Babylon, having been part of the first major round of

16. Cook, "Ezekiel."
17. Kutsko, *Between Heaven and Earth*, 92.

deportations in 597 BCE. As the story is told in 2 Kings 24, when King Nebuchadnezzar of Babylon besieged Jerusalem in 597, King Jehoiachin of Judah surrendered himself and his family to the invading king, who took them and some number of Judahites into exile. Nebuchadnezzar also reportedly took with him the treasures of the palace and the cultic implements from the temple. Then, after the Babylon-appointed king Zedekiah rebels against Babylon, Nebuchadnezzar returns in 587 BCE to besiege Jerusalem again, starving its residents, blinding and deporting the king, carrying more people into exile, absconding with the temple's remaining treasures, and burning the city, including both the king's house and the house of God. The theological crisis for a Zadokite priest steeped in Zion theology is readily apparent: If God has chosen the Davidic kings to rule in Jerusalem, where God himself sits enthroned on the cherubim with the ark of the covenant as his footstool, and now the palace and temple have been looted and then lost to a foreign invading force, *where is God*? Why have the promises been lost, and is God now anywhere to be found?

Ezekiel's First Vision

Hints of Ezekiel's new evaluation of theological assumptions are already apparent in the vision that opens the book. He sees four creatures, perhaps some version of the winged cherubim that flank the divine throne (Exod. 25:18–22) but with four faces each. Each creature accompanies a wheel with rims full of eyes. The text emphasizes the mobility of these wheels, noting that the wheels could move in any direction "without veering." In my mind this smooth change in direction is akin to the movement of a spinner suitcase, or any other swivel-wheel mechanism, where the direction can be changed instantly, without stopping to pivot. The text dwells on the movement of the wheels and the creatures: "When the living creatures moved, the wheels moved beside them; and when the living creatures rose from the earth, the wheels rose.

Wherever the spirit would go, they went, and the wheels rose along with them; for the spirit of the living creatures was in the wheels. When they moved, the others moved; when they stopped, the others stopped; and when they rose from the earth, the wheels rose along with them; for the spirit of the living creatures was in the wheels" (Ezek. 1:19–21). Above the heads of the creatures is "something like a dome" (v. 22), and above the dome is "something like a throne," on which is seated "something that seemed like a human form" (v. 26), again with "something that looked like fire" and splendor surrounding it (v. 27). Ezekiel explains, "Like the bow in a cloud on a rainy day, such was the appearance of the splendor all around. This was the appearance of the likeness of the glory of the LORD" (v. 28a).

Ezekiel's vision is vivid, and yet the language he uses to describe it is faltering, leaning on simile and approximation. Everything he sees is "something like" a recognizable form but not quite the thing itself. Moreover, from Ezekiel's vantage point below the wheels, the full import of this grand vehicle is difficult to grasp at first. As Cook notes, "God's presence is removed from the prophet by a graduated, spatial system of tiered holiness with wheels, monsters, and a crystalline expanse demarcating the storied levels."[18] Throughout Ezekiel we can observe this paradoxical tension between God's nearness and God's distance, God's presence and God's absence, as the prophet himself works out whether God's presence will ever be known to the people cast out of the land.[19]

Journey of the Glory of God

Ezekiel's initial vision establishes both the mobility of the divine throne and God's will and ability to be encountered outside

---

18. Cook, "Ezekiel," 244.
19. Cf. Kutsko, *Between Heaven and Earth*, whose study on the paradox of divine presence and absence in Ezekiel teases out the ways in which "exile is both a means of punishment and an opportunity for divine presence" (94).

of the temple—indeed, outside of Jerusalem and Judah altogether. These divine characteristics already signal a shift in theological thinking. As Cook remarks, "The thought that God's throne could appear in Babylonia, over five hundred miles from God's holy city of Jerusalem, must have required a major psychological adjustment for Ezekiel."[20] With these new ideas about divine travel laid out, the glory of God goes on a journey through the rest of the book of Ezekiel. This journey is not a straightforward narrative with the divine glory as its protagonist; instead, moments within Ezekiel's larger visions of judgment and, ultimately, restoration serve as structural and thematic touchstones for the shape of the book as a whole.[21]

After Ezekiel has been commissioned by God for his work, having famously eaten the scroll of lamentation that tasted "sweet as honey" (Ezek. 2:8–3:3), the prophet goes back to his fellow exiles at Tel-abib, a town in Babylonia near the river Chebar, where he had experienced his first vision. He is conveyed there either by or alongside the divine chariot (3:12–15). After prophesying there, he goes out to a nearby valley, and there he sees the glory of the LORD as he had seen it at Chebar (3:22–23). After several symbolic acts and prophecies of destruction, the text describes how Ezekiel is again lifted up and moved, this time by a gleaming, fiery figure: "It stretched out the form of a hand, and took me by a lock of my head; and the spirit lifted me up between earth and heaven, and brought me in visions of God to Jerusalem, to the entrance of the gateway of the inner court that faces north, to the seat of the image of the jealousy, which provokes to jealousy. And the glory of the God of Israel was there, like the vision that I had seen in the valley" (8:3–4). God takes Ezekiel on a tour of all the "abominations" happening at the temple, including idols installed along the walls and the worship of other gods—a cumulative

---

20. Cook, "Ezekiel," 245.
21. Cook, "Ezekiel," 244; Kutsko, *Between Heaven and Earth*.

mishmash of decades of apostate practices, many of which are decried in 1 and 2 Kings. God describes these practices as "the great abominations that the house of Israel are committing here, to drive me far from my sanctuary" (8:6). Israel's infidelities to Yahweh are marked as the cause of the departure of God's glory from the temple.

As the instructions in Ezekiel's visions continue, the glory of the LORD moves to the threshold of the temple (Ezek. 9:3; 10:4–5) and then to the east gate of the temple's outer court (10:19). Ezekiel repeatedly confirms that this is the same vehicle from his very first vision, now identifying the four creatures on the chariot specifically as cherubim (10:20). The spatial orientation of this journey continues to face east, the direction of Babylon. Finally, in chapter 11, having left the temple, the glory of the LORD leaves Jerusalem altogether: "Then the cherubim lifted up their wings, with the wheels beside them; and the glory of the God of Israel was above them. And the glory of the LORD ascended from the middle of the city, and stopped on the mountain east of the city" (11:22–23). The visions and oracles of judgment that have permeated Ezekiel so far are punctuated by the gradual movement of the glory out of the city.

At this point in the chronology of the book of Ezekiel, it appears that the Jerusalem temple is still standing. However, at Ezekiel 33:21 word reaches the prophet that Jerusalem has fallen completely to the Babylonians. This marks a pivot point in Ezekiel's career. The judgment he has been proclaiming that God will visit on all Israel, not especially the exiles, has arrived. The promised nadir is here, the prophet is vindicated, and now he can turn to words of hope. The climax of this hope is Ezekiel's vision of the new temple, and indeed a new Israel, spanning chapters 40–48.

Having been taken on a brief tour of the abominations that had hijacked the first temple (Ezek. 8:1–18), Ezekiel is now taken by a heavenly guide on an extended tour of the new temple. After making their way through, measuring all along, they arrive at the east gate, where God's glory had departed the temple in chapters 10–11. Now the glory returns.

> Then he brought me to the gate, the gate facing east. And there, the glory of the God of Israel was coming from the east; the sound was like the sound of mighty waters; and the earth shone with his glory. The vision I saw was like the vision that I had seen when he came to destroy the city, and like the vision that I had seen by the river Chebar; and I fell upon my face. As the glory of the LORD entered the temple by the gate facing east, the spirit lifted me up, and brought me into the inner court; and the glory of the LORD filled the temple.
>
> While the man was standing beside me, I heard someone speaking to me out of the temple. He said to me: Mortal, this is the place of my throne and the place for the soles of my feet, where I will reside among the people of Israel forever. . . . Now let them put away their idolatry and the corpses of their kings far from me, and I will reside among them forever. (43:1–7a, 9)

Ezekiel and his guide eventually move to survey the land of Israel more broadly. The prophet receives new instructions for dividing the land among the tribes, and the city gates receive their measurements and new names. Finally, the closing words of the book of Ezekiel give a name to this new city, this new Jerusalem: *Yahweh-shammah*, "The LORD Is There" (48:35). The city will be known to all precisely by God's presence within it. God can be anywhere; God wants to be, and will be, dwelling in a newly sanctified—in fact, an altogether new—Jerusalem.

This final vision is really more than a depiction of the temple's restoration. As Katheryn Pfisterer Darr puts it, "In his fourth and final vision report, Ezekiel describes a perfectly ordered Israelite society living in a perfectly ordered homeland under the leadership of a perfectly ordered priesthood serving in a perfectly ordered Temple complex."[22] Although the detailed specifications of the

---

22. Darr, *Book of Ezekiel*, 6:1532.

temple space will recall for the reader of Exodus the tabernacle instructions that close out that book, Ezekiel's report is less a set of instructions and more an idealized possibility. Again with Darr's delightful turn of phrase, "The devil is *not* in the details! The details make possible God's abiding presence."[23] Holy space itself is no longer confined to the temple but spills out into creation.

Ezekiel's Theological Reckoning

We posed this age-old question at the start: In times of profound disaster, *where can God be found*? So how, in the end, has Ezekiel answered it? And where is God to be found in the best circumstances? On the one hand, the journey of God's glory in Ezekiel affirms that the temple is the proper dwelling place for God. Exile has not shaken Ezekiel's commitment to priestly values; if anything, he has doubled down on them by embracing a holiness perspective that requires holiness from all the people and sees holiness in all the land. God's absence from the temple is the fault of the people, who have driven God away from the sanctuary by their apostasies and who will receive God's righteous judgment. The temple is where God ought to be, and it is where God will be when things are set right.

On the other hand, Ezekiel dispels any possible notions that God is *confined* to the temple. Over and over again, the prophet witnesses the presence of God in exile with him. God is on the move, riding that divine chariot in any direction God wishes. The throne itself connotes a resting place for God, and yet that resting place is on wheels, ready to roll wherever the glory needs to roll. This is a profound rethinking of the Zion theology that flourished in the Zadokite priesthood. Yet at the end of the day, it is also an affirmation of it. The book of Ezekiel reckons with tradition, holding it close yet also being open to Spirit-led feats of imagination that envision new ways forward.

23. Darr, *Book of Ezekiel*, 6:1534.

Ezekiel Today

It can be difficult to know what to do with the book of Ezekiel today. Although it is a favorite text for a few readers attempting to decode the Bible for signs of the end times, most of us are at a loss for how to make sense of its visions, which are, on the one hand, strange and fantastical and, on the other hand, so deeply rooted in a particular and identifiable historical context—the Babylonian exile—that their relevance is difficult to identify. The profoundly problematic metaphors of violence against women, especially egregious in chapters 16 and 23, further complicate Ezekiel's legacy. Is there anything about this book that "translates" for twenty-first-century Christians? Even with all these caveats, there are, I daresay, many ways Ezekiel intersects with our modern lives. I will explore two possibilities here before considering Ezekiel and Deuteronomy together as testimonies toward theological dynamism in the Old Testament.

First, Ezekiel, like all the priestly texts with which he has an affinity, asks us to ponder where we see *holy space*. The coronavirus pandemic of 2020 undeniably laid bare questions about the purpose and methods of Christian worship, questions with which Christians wrestled all around the world. When gathering together in community was suddenly unsafe, a suspension of in-person church services prompted reflection on the relationship of worship to space and place. And while few would claim that God is wholly inaccessible outside the church doors, choosing to gather or not gather became contested measures of holiness. Even so, the pandemic did not suddenly introduce holy space as a complex issue for the church. That has been a recurring topic since the first church buildings were designed, and it has become particularly acute in the last few decades, as some churches struggle to meet their building budgets, others build theaters for worship spaces in lieu of traditional sanctuaries, and still others convert their worship spaces into mission-driven social enterprises.

The book of Ezekiel is also an important reminder of the *limitations of language* when we seek to speak about God. "Theology" at its most literal is exactly that—*speech about God* (Greek *theos*, meaning "God," and *logia*, meaning "speech")—yet to represent God by either words or images is always a fraught undertaking. This is evident in the halting language Ezekiel uses to describe his opening vision: "*something like* a dome," "*something like* a human form*," and so on. It is also affirmed in Ezekiel's own speechlessness, which recurs on and off until the destruction of the temple loosens his tongue. The fantastic nature of many of the visions themselves is also puzzling, approximate. The imagery showcases the paradox of God's palpable nearness and yet God's complete otherness.[24] The glory of God is at once too dazzling to comprehend and too faithful to shake off. These linguistic limitations and puzzling paradoxes can at times be frustrating, but I also find them to be a source of immense hope. Ezekiel helps us see how the mysteries of God are also part of the majesty of God. Experience of the absence of God is as much a part of biblical tradition as the experience of direct encounters with God.[25] And yet Ezekiel offers hope that even when God seems utterly indiscernible to us, God remains near.

Rethinking Theology

Our forays into Deuteronomy and Ezekiel have underscored yet again the multivocal nature of the Hebrew Bible. Scripture preserves contrasting ideas about any number of topics. Yet in these two particular cases, that multivocity does not comprise different

---

24. Cf. Cook, "Ezekiel," 244–45.
25. Biblical laments, such as the lament psalms and the book of Lamentations, are another rich source of biblical reckonings with God's potential absence. In ancient Israel's darkest hour, in the depths of the siege of Jerusalem, the poet of Lamentations allows the specter of God's abandonment to surface and even to linger as the last possibility voiced in the poem (Lam. 5:22).

ideas sitting side by side but rather reflects deliberate reevaluation of existing theological expectations. Deuteronomy supplants existing cultic regulations allowing animal slaughter at local sanctuaries with a program of centralized worship, a change that also requires, among other things, explicitly allowing secular slaughter. Ezekiel reexamines the dearly held understanding that the Jerusalem temple is the place to encounter God, concluding that God can be anywhere, even in exile, but also that God desires to return to God's temple dwelling in a renewed, holy land.

Of course, the texts preserved in the Bible do not represent the totality of experiences in ancient Judah. Both Deuteronomy and Ezekiel reflect very particular ideologies representing very particular groups in ancient Israel at very particular times. Deuteronomy reflects the interests of the scribes enmeshed with the monarchy in the late seventh century BCE, when the threat from Assyria seems to be waning and Babylonian power has not yet been discovered looming on the horizon. Ezekiel reflects the interests of the Zadokite priesthood, also heavily invested in the monarchy, when that institution is about to crumble. Each innovates in order to address what *for their social group* is a pressing theo-political issue. It is never self-evident whether those motives are "pure" or whether those innovations are the "right" thing to do; those evaluations are left to each interpreter. Just to note that a theology—ancient or modern—has been rethought does not automatically mean that it has been reconceived for the better. But what we can certainly affirm is that theological innovation is not off-limits in the Bible; on the contrary, it is woven into the fabric of the Bible.

The lived experiences of faithful people require ongoing reorientation of our understanding of who God is, what God requires of us, where God can be found, and how we can best live in relationship with God. That is not to say that there can be no immovable foundations on which we can build that faith, although they will differ among traditions and among interpreters within a tradition.[26] Even so, part of the dynamism of the biblical witness is that it demonstrates theological puzzling, a flexibility to reimagine new possibilities when the order of the world as we know it begins to crack. In a complex world, the Old Testament offers examples of creativity amid crisis. In the next chapter we will see just how creative the biblical writers could get in the face of great catastrophe, as we return to the book of Daniel to investigate apocalyptic literature.

---

26. For example, as a product of the Reformed tradition, I confess Jesus as the living Word revealed through Scripture and as the lens through which all interpretation should proceed. But even what I mean by those ideas still stems from, and is subject to, acts of interpretation. For more on theological hermeneutics and the inevitability of interpretation, see Caputo, *Hermeneutics*.

4

Developing a New Genre

The Rise of the Apocalypse

The preceding chapters have emphasized that the Bible contains many different types of texts and that those texts date from many different moments across the span of ancient Israelite history. Many of the genres of literature attested in the Hebrew Bible, such as the flood account in Genesis 6–9, exhibit significant continuities with existing literature from the ancient Near East. Often a single story has been pieced together from multiple sources spanning hundreds of years. Biblical authors reworked their own older traditions, as well as those of their neighbors, to make new claims in the face of changing historical, political, and theological circumstances.

The Bible's reliance on and interactions with existing traditions from surrounding cultures can hardly be overstated. Nevertheless, the Old Testament is also marked with innovations that are by and large unique to ancient Jewish literary traditions. Chief among them is the apocalypse, a new genre of literature that arose in the third and second centuries BCE, a time of significant upheaval for the Jewish community in Judea.

The popular use of the word "apocalypse" today implies an *event*, usually the end of the world or a cataclysmic, supernatural battle with global repercussions. In the realm of biblical studies, however, an apocalypse is a *literary genre* in which hidden, divine knowledge is said to be revealed to a human intermediary. The Greek word *apokalypsis* itself means "unveiling" or "revelation." If there is an event inherent in an apocalypse, it is first and foremost a transfer of knowledge, rather than an epic battle. Apocalypses use language that is highly symbolic, and they interpret earthly events in terms of supernatural ones. Apocalypses often do look toward the end of the world, though that is not an essential component of the genre.[1] Even so, apocalypses still concern themselves broadly with "eschatology," the "end" of things—if not the world overall, then at least the "fate of the dead."[2] The idea of the resurrection of the dead, for example, is absent from most of the Old Testament but does appear in Daniel 12.

Perhaps the most famous biblical apocalypse is the New Testament book of Revelation. The opening sentences of the book are particularly helpful for orienting us to the genre: "A revelation [Greek *apokalypsis*] of Jesus Christ, which God gave him to show his servants what must soon take place. Christ made it known by sending it through his angel to his servant John, who bore witness to the word of God and to the witness of Jesus Christ, including all that John saw" (Rev. 1:1–2 CEB). Divine knowledge is passed from Jesus—who in turn had received it from God—to John via an angel, the mediator of the message between the divine and the human. The vision is forward looking—regarding "what must soon take place"—and yet it will present that interpretation of the future by means of extensive commentary on the present.

In the Hebrew Bible, the most fully developed apocalypse is found in the last six chapters of the book of Daniel. Several snip-

---

1. Hanson, "Apocalypses and Apocalypticism."
2. Collins, "What Is Apocalyptic Literature?," 5.

pets of other books can also be described as "apocalyptic"—that is, sharing a worldview that overlaps with the primary interests of the apocalypses. These Old Testament texts include Isaiah 24–27, Isaiah 56–66, Ezekiel 38–39, and much of Zechariah. Yet most Jewish apocalypses from the Second Temple period exist outside the biblical canon, such as 1 and 2 Enoch, 2 and 3 Baruch, 4 Ezra, and the Apocalypse of Abraham, among others.[3] Thus while we will limit our discussion to the Daniel apocalypse within the canonical text of the Hebrew Bible, it is important to acknowledge that the apocalypse is by no means a purely biblical phenomenon, limited only to material deemed canonical in Jewish or Christian tradition. Rather, apocalypses are features of literary activity, broadly conceived, in Second Temple Judaism and early Christianity. Only a fraction of that literary activity was eventually collected into the Bible.

Despite our emphasis on the newness and uniqueness of the apocalypse in its heyday, we must also acknowledge that the genre did not appear on the Second Temple literary scene completely out of nowhere. The idea that an earthly messenger is mediating a communication from God is essentially the baseline definition of prophecy, and some scholars view apocalyptic literature as a phenomenon rooted in and organically developing from the postexilic prophetic tradition. Other scholars have posited that the dualism between good and evil prominent in many apocalypses must be dependent on Persian Zoroastrian material. Akkadian prophecies originating in Mesopotamia share some characteristics with apocalypses, and some apocalypses allude to mythic material from Ugarit or Babylon. Parallels can also be identified with Hellenistic political prophecy.[4] Apocalyptic literature both emerges

---

3. For the text of these and other Second Temple apocalyptic works, see Charlesworth, *Old Testament Pseudepigrapha*, vol. 1.

4. See Collins, *Apocalyptic Imagination*, 26–47, for a review of scholarship on the potential historical and cross-cultural influences on apocalyptic literature. Cf. Collins, "What Is Apocalyptic Literature?," 8–9.

from and draws upon the literary forms and theological insights that preceded it. Nevertheless, unlike the biblical creation and flood stories or even the court stories, early Jewish apocalypses have no clear, direct antecedent in a single stream of tradition. We can thus be confident in naming the early Jewish apocalypse as an innovation in and for its time.

Apocalyptic literature is also an innovation *within* Jewish tradition. As John Collins affirms, "In fact, both the literary genre and the worldview that it articulated were quite novel in ancient Judaism, and stand in sharp contrast to the traditional worldview of covenantal nomism."[5] In other words, apocalyptic thought within ancient Judaism gave less attention to covenant and law and instead emphasized cosmic order and eschatological hope. Judaism in the Second Temple period was by no means monolithic, and the framework of apocalyptic eschatology may not have been embraced across all the diverse manifestations of Jewish thought and practice. Nevertheless, scholars have shown that the apocalyptic literature in 1 and 2 Enoch in particular was a significant part of Second Temple Judaism, conversant with and arising alongside the texts we now regard as canonical.[6]

Apocalypses can be classified into two subgroups: the "historical apocalypses," which tend to focus on an overview of history revealed by means of visions, and the "otherworldly journeys," in which the messenger of the divine revelation takes the human recipient on a tour of the cosmos. The Daniel apocalypses are of the historical variety, as are the other early Jewish apocalypses roughly contemporaneous with it: the Apocalypse of Weeks (1 En. 93:1–10; 91:11–17) and the Book of Dreams (1 En. 83–90), both found within 1 Enoch, a composite collection of several apocalypses.[7]

---

5. Collins, "What Is Apocalyptic Literature?," 7.
6. See the extensive discussion, including in the notes, on the Enochic tradition and its place alongside covenantal tradition in Second Temple Judaism in Portier-Young, *Apocalypse against Empire*, 280–312.
7. Nickelsburg and VanderKam, *1 Enoch*.

The Book of the Watchers (1 En. 1–36) and the Astronomical Book (1 En. 72–82), also from the Enochic tradition, predate the apocalypses of Daniel 7–12, which means that the canonical biblical text does not provide the first example of the genre. Like Daniel, the Apocalypse of Weeks, and the Book of Dreams, the earlier apocalypses also reflect a sense of crisis, but because they provide few historical touchstones, the exact nature of the crisis is difficult to identify, beyond general "violence and lawlessness" in Hellenistic Judea.[8] In Daniel and the contemporaneous Enochic literature, though, the crisis that births their visions is clear: the direct, targeted persecutions of Jews in Judea under the reign of Antiochus IV Epiphanes.

Judea under Antiochus

The sixth century BCE marked a particularly chaotic time in the life of ancient Israel. The fall of Jerusalem, destruction of the temple, and exile of Israel's elites to Babylon sparked a theological crisis, requiring a reevaluation of core claims. Moreover, the Babylonian exile marked the beginning of a new era of imperial domination over Israel. Although Cyrus authorized the exiles to return to Judah and rebuild the temple in Jerusalem, Persia's beneficence was limited; Judah remained a Persian colony. The hope that marked the sweeping endorsements of Cyrus in Isaiah 40–55 eroded as the depth of Persia's domination, particularly in economic terms, became clearer (Neh. 9:36–37).

In 332 BCE, Alexander the Great defeated Persia and assumed control of Judah. At first, Greek rule looked a lot like Persian rule; Alexander kept many of his predecessors' policies in place. However, just eight years later Alexander died, and control of the lands he had conquered was divided between his generals,

---

8. Collins, *Apocalyptic Imagination*, 61–65. See also Williamson and Schedtler, "Apocalyptic Movements in Early Judaism," 100–101.

the Diadochi ("successors"). Judah—referred to as Judea in this period—was initially ruled by the dynasty of Ptolemy, who held many of Alexander's western territories. In the east, a Macedonian general named Seleucus was establishing his own dynasty, conquering Babylon and its surrounding regions. When Ptolemy failed to join a coalition of Diadochi fighting against Antigonus, a rival Macedonian general, the region of Coele-Syria (the Greek name for Syria-Palestine) was given to Seleucus by the coalition.[9] The dispute over the territory set off decades upon decades of conflict. As Anathea Portier-Young writes, "Although the Ptolemies maintained control of the region for a century, the warrior kings of the Ptolemaic and Seleucid dynasties never ceased to battle and jockey for dominion over Coele-Syria. As a result, inhabitants of Coele-Syria, including the Judeans, suffered through no fewer than six 'Syrian wars' waged on their land by the Ptolemies and Seleucids between the years 274 and 168 BCE. By contrast with the two centuries of Persian rule that preceded it, the Hellenistic era was a time of almost ceaseless violence for Judeans."[10]

Armed struggles in the region were accompanied by political ones. The allegiances of Judeans were divided between those loyal to Ptolemy and those who opposed his rule. Ptolemaic administrative policies eliminated the role of the provincial governor and increased the influence of the high priest and of aristocratic families. Key to this shift was the system of "tax farming" introduced by the Ptolemies, in which the job of tax collecting was sold at auction. Winning bidders would collect extra taxes both to find favor with the Ptolemies and to provide their own revenue.[11] This practice drove taxes higher and bred resentment among the local populations in Palestine, resentment that was "directed not only toward the Ptolemaic government but also toward those natives

---

9. Hayes and Mandell, *Jewish People in Classical Antiquity*, 29–30.
10. Portier-Young, *Apocalypse against Empire*, 55.
11. Hayes and Mandell, *Jewish People in Classical Antiquity*, 34–35; Newsom, *Daniel: A Commentary*, 23–28.

who were tax farmers and thus considered to be arms and instruments of the foreign oppressors."[12] Thus the third and early second centuries BCE introduced significant new stressors for the Jewish community in Judea in the forms of extensive political conflict, burgeoning economic hardship, and ongoing violence.

As significant as these stressors were, circumstances for Jews in Palestine turned particularly dire with the rise to power of Antiochus IV Epiphanes. The Seleucids gained control of Judea during the fifth Syrian war, and Antiochus assumed the throne in 175 BCE, positioning himself through much manipulation as the new king following the assassination of his older brother, Seleucus IV. Conflict in Judea continued to fester, particularly between factions loyal to Jason, a former high priest, and Menelaus, who had wrested the position away from him. Around 169 BCE, while Antiochus was carrying out military campaigns in Egypt, Jason attempted to take control of Jerusalem by force, having heard an incorrect rumor that Antiochus was dead (2 Macc. 5:5). Antiochus returned from Egypt to put down the rebellion with significant violence, including plundering the temple. Two years later, Antiochus sent a commander named Apollonius to Jerusalem, again to put down unrest, this time with an even more forceful hand. In the wake of these invasions, Antiochus instituted a program of persecutions against the Jews that included violence, torture, and an unprecedented level of religious desecration.

The books of 1 and 2 Maccabees, found in the Apocrypha, report Antiochus's acts of oppression, sometimes in graphic detail.[13] When Antiochus returned from his second invasion of Egypt, the

12. Hayes and Mandell, *Jewish People in Classical Antiquity*, 35.
13. First Maccabees is particularly driven by pro-Hasmonean loyalties, and, as with any historical text, we should not automatically assume it is without bias or embellishment in its account. Yet even if some of the details were shown to be overdrawn, the testimony of the text overwhelmingly points to a significant experience of persecution for Jews in Judea. For more on the sources for reconstructing the history of the Maccabean revolt, see Hayes and Mandell, *Jewish People in Classical Antiquity*, 47–49.

text describes "massacre of young and old, destruction of boys, women, and children, and slaughter of young girls and infants. Within the total of three days, eighty thousand were destroyed, forty thousand in hand-to-hand fighting, and as many were sold into slavery as were killed" (2 Macc. 5:13–14). While ferocity in putting down rebellions or unrest was no innovation, Antiochus's particular focus on Jewish practices and identifiers was a marked departure from the more relaxed approach to religion adopted by his predecessors.[14] Circumcision was outlawed, and circumcised boys and their mothers were executed (1 Macc. 1:60–61; 2 Macc. 6:10). The Jerusalem temple was rededicated as a temple of Zeus and polluted by offerings of swine on its altar (1 Macc. 1:54–59; 2 Macc. 6:1–6). Torah scrolls were destroyed (1 Macc. 1:56). Martyrs endured torture before death, including scalping, burning, and mutilation, rather than eat swine's flesh or offer unclean sacrifices (1 Macc. 1:63; 2 Macc. 6:7–7:42).

In her analysis of Antiochus's reign of terror, Portier-Young emphasizes that, despite the novelty of his religious tyranny, Antiochus's edict against the Jews was nonetheless consistent with his overall "program of conquest and creation," which was to override Jews' claims to the sovereignty of God and substitute Antiochus's own sovereign power: "Antiochus aimed through his edict and persecution at the unmaking and making of world and identity for the inhabitants of Judea in order to assert the empire as sole power, reality, and ground of being. Antiochus himself would emerge as its creator and as true author (and authorizer) of identity."[15] Thus Jews in the Hellenistic era faced a crisis that was neither fleeting nor incidental. Instead, responding to the persecutions of Antiochus required a radical reassessment of life under empire and under God.

14. As Newsom notes, "Persecution for religious reasons was basically unknown in Hellenistic culture" (*Daniel: A Commentary*, 27). Cf. Portier-Young, *Apocalypse against Empire*, 175.

15. Portier-Young, *Apocalypse against Empire*, 178.

Apocalypse in Daniel

Even the most casual reader of the Hebrew Bible will intuit a difference in Daniel 7–12 from the chapters that precede it as well as from the other books that surround it. Its highly symbolic language, its bold and strange imagery, its concern for eschatology, and the first-person presentation of Daniel's visions set this section of the book apart from other texts. Like the book of Revelation, Daniel 7–12 can be a source of both fascination and dread in Christian communities today, with readers wondering whether its devouring beasts and epic battles are portents for times to come.

While any predictions of a future end of days are perennially murky, clear references to the past dominate the Daniel apocalypse. Many details in Daniel can be identified as touchpoints connecting the book's visions with particular historical realities under the reign of Antiochus; indeed, the terror of the visions matches the terror of that moment. Here we will look at Daniel 8 as a representative example of that imagery.

Daniel 8 and Monstrous Symbols

Daniel 8 is written in Hebrew, shifting back to that language after the Aramaic of chapters 2–7. Though composed in the middle of the Antiochene persecutions, the chapter is set during the reign of King Belshazzar of Babylon, who had served as the antagonist of chapter 5, in dread of the writing on the wall at his royal banquet. The effect is to give Daniel's visions a predictive feel, even as they comment on current—that is, second-century—events.

Daniel has a vision in which he is standing by a river in the Persian capital Susa. A ram with two horns stands beside the river and then charges to the west, south, and north, growing stronger all the time. A goat with a single horn between its eyes charges the ram, breaking its horns and trampling it. The goat's own horn then breaks, giving way to four new horns, one of which sprouts another, smaller horn. That smaller horn immediately grows large and not only wreaks havoc on earth but also turns its destructive force toward the heavens: "It threw down to the earth some of the host [of heaven] and some of the stars, and trampled on them" (Dan. 8:10). The horn then turns to the sanctuary to desecrate it. As Daniel tries to make sense of this vision, the messenger Gabriel appears to him and offers an interpretation of it.

Gabriel informs Daniel that the ram with the two horns represents the kings of Media and Persia, and the goat is the king of Greece. Its first, big horn is the "first king" (i.e., Alexander) and then the four subsequent horns represent the "four kingdoms" (that is, the reigns of the Diadochi, the generals among whom Alexander's kingdom was divided after his death). After the four kingdoms subside, a "king of bold countenance shall arise" (Dan. 8:23), who will prosper in destruction against people and God until "he shall be broken, and not by human hands" (v. 25). We can quite safely assume this refers to Antiochus IV Epiphanes, though he is never explicitly named in the text.

Indeed, this explanation and the vision that preceded it are at once mysteriously vague and astonishingly specific. The text refrains from using the names of any of the kings, but it does name places. It uses cardinal directions that map accurately to the conquests of the rulers in question, and it describes apostasies in the sanctuary that align with the desecrations by Antiochus. A reader in second-century Judea surely would have known the references and would have seen their own experience of history affirmed. Yet the chapter also uses very generalized language; for example, the notion that "in his own mind he shall be great" is applicable to most despots throughout history (Dan. 8:25). The future-oriented language—"it refers to many days from now" (v. 26)—leaves the timeline for the fulfillment open ended. Even references that seem to point to God use neither the name of God nor a common word or title, instead referring to "the prince of the host" (v. 11) or "the Prince of princes" (v. 25). Moreover, Daniel himself despairs that he does not understand the vision, leaving the impression for the reader that there may be more to it than even what is communicated by Gabriel. The cumulative effect of this combination of details and generalizations is to leave the vision of Daniel 8 open for reinterpretation and reemployment in future ages, even as it also remains grounded in the events of the second century BCE.

Time and the End of Time

Jarring symbolism is only one part of Daniel's apocalyptic rhetoric. Daniel 7–12 also underlines the finitude of the current era of suffering by undertaking a periodization of history, in which power is given over to oppressive forces for fixed intervals according to the decrees of God. Keeping with the pattern of apocalyptic discourse, those times are specified—but in mysterious or symbolic language so they still are not yet clear. Take, for example, this passage from Daniel 9:

> Seventy weeks are decreed for your people and your holy city: to finish the transgression, to put an end to sin, and to atone for iniquity, to bring in everlasting righteousness, to seal both vision and prophet, and to anoint a most holy place. Know therefore and understand: from the time that the word went out to restore and rebuild Jerusalem until the time of an anointed prince, there shall be seven weeks; and for sixty-two weeks it shall be built again with streets and moat, but in a troubled time. (vv. 24–25)

At the outset of the chapter, Daniel has been puzzling over Jeremiah's prophecy that Jerusalem's desolation will be fulfilled after seventy years (9:2). Gabriel informs Daniel that the time is not seventy years but seventy "weeks of years"—that is, 490 years. This adjustment of Jeremiah expands upon the earlier tradition and participates further in the imparting of hidden knowledge to Daniel and, through him, to the reader. Similar patterns of the language of "weeks" are noted in the early Enochic literature so that the chapter draws on both the well-known biblical tradition and the Enochic tradition (which was vibrant in the Second Temple period but, as it lies outside of the canon, tends to be less well known today).[16] The vision goes on to specify the other occurrences that will precede the time when "the decreed end is poured out upon the desolator" (v. 27b). In this example of periodization, the crisis that is predicted—that is, underway—is revealed to be part of God's providential control over all of history.

As the book of Daniel draws to a close, Daniel's visions move further toward the eschaton, the end of *all* things, not just of Antiochus's persecutions. Like several other of Daniel's visions, the revealed scene beginning at Daniel 12:5 takes place beside a body of water. Daniel sees divine messengers, including one clothed in linen, evocative of the temple priesthood. He hears the messengers discussing the time until the end of days, which will include the "wonders" of anguish, deliverance, and resurrection (vv. 1–3). As readers, we are invited to overhear with him.

> Then I, Daniel, looked, and two others appeared, one standing on this bank of the stream and one on the other. One of them said to the man clothed in linen, who was upstream, "How long shall it be until the end of these wonders?" The man clothed in linen, who was upstream, raised his right hand and his left hand toward heaven. And I heard him swear by the one who lives forever that it would be for a time, two times, and half a time, and that when the shattering of the power of the holy people comes to an end, all these things would be accomplished. I heard but could not understand. (vv. 5–8a)

The revelation of divine knowledge is the organizational backbone of these apocalypses. Alongside the category of revelation is divine control over history and time. By predicting "a time, two times, and half a time," the vision communicates a confident specificity

16. Newsom, *Daniel: A Commentary*, 299–303.

and yet also a generative ambiguity. That even Daniel, the primary recipient of this special knowledge, remains befuddled means that we, the readers, can find comfort in our confusion.

Functions of Apocalypse

We saw in chapter 2 that the court tales in Daniel 1–6 have inspired much scholarly debate over whether the tales promote accommodation to the empire or resistance to it. In Daniel 7–12 the scales tip more decisively toward resistance. There is no going along to get along. There is no persuading the little horn to temperance with a show of piety. This "contemptible person" (Dan. 11:21), Antiochus, will ravage the land, its people, and God's temple. Yet the visions promise that the sufferings will eventually come to an end and the wise and righteous will be vindicated. The question before us in Daniel 7–12, then, is more about the *nature* of this resistance. Is the apocalypse a call to arms, perhaps to join the Maccabean revolt? Is it an escapist vision that waits for God to defeat Antiochus? Or is it something else entirely?

Portier-Young has argued convincingly that the very creation of the symbolic world in second-century apocalypses resists the totalizing claims of Antiochus's empire. She writes:

> The apocalyptic writers sought to expose the imperial spectacle as a deceptive and monstrous negation of life. They redirected attention from empire's chaos to the divine throne, heavenly worship, a future earthly temple, and books of truth, revealing God's plan for deliverance and judgment and a new just order to come. . . . They developed new symbols and language to transform memory, resisting the fragmentation of self and time through a new visionary form that reconnected past, present, and future in a narrative governed by divine providence. In these ways *apocalypse intervened in the logic of terror* and so countered the empire's deadliest weapon.[17]

---

17. Portier-Young, *Apocalypse against Empire*, 175 (emphasis added).

For the authors of the Apocalypse of Weeks and the Book of Dreams, texts in 1 Enoch that are roughly contemporaneous with Daniel, armed resistance fighting for and with God was on the horizon. By contrast, the Danielic author(s) looked to the hosts of heaven to do the fighting, and they instead advocated "nonviolent resistance and covenant obedience."[18] Yet in both of these apocalyptic traditions, the texts claim God's ultimate control over the oppressive powers of the world.

A common and long-standing assumption about the strange symbolism of Daniel's apocalypse is that such imagery is a kind of secret code, one that might provide a safe cover for the oppressed as they share hopeful visions of the overthrow of their oppressors. Already in our brief investigation into Daniel 8 we have seen evidence against this proposal—namely, that Gabriel offers some specifics about the vision to help Daniel (and the reader) understand it. Even if Antiochus is not explicitly named, identifying the goat as the king of Greece would not be particularly effective at masking the second-century referents of these symbols.[19]

Perhaps, then, the symbolic world of the apocalypse does not mean to keep readers out but rather to welcome readers in. Carol Newsom emphasizes that the Daniel apocalypses use "epiphanic rhetoric" to attempt to persuade their audience that God exerts control over history: "To do this, they construct a palpable sense of reality, cause the reader to desire access to that reality, and construct the seer as a figure of authority who mediates that access. They also construct the audience as persons who are like the seer himself in important respects."[20] Rather than a code to be deciphered, apocalypse is a world to be entered. It creates a space where the chaos of reality is reframed as a world of divine

---

18. Portier-Young, *Apocalypse against Empire*, 219.

19. Cf. the discussion of pseudonymous authorship in Portier-Young, *Apocalypse against Empire*, 31–43.

20. Newsom, *Daniel: A Commentary*, 19.

power and mystery, in which the reader is invited to receive and be empowered by its hidden knowledge.[21]

Apocalypse after Antiochus

Even as the persecutions of Antiochus raged, Judas Maccabeus was building an armed rebellion against the Seleucid Empire and against Menelaus, the high priest appointed by Antiochus whom many viewed as complicit in his terror.[22] Taking advantage of Antiochus's absence fighting the Parthians in the east, Judas and his Hasmonean forces won multiple battles in the struggle for control of Jerusalem. In December 164 BCE, they took control of the temple, purified it, rebuilt its altar, and restored its daily sacrificial practices. Around this same time, Antiochus IV died while away on a military campaign, and his son and successor Antiochus V was ready to restore control of the temple to the Jews (2 Macc. 11:22–26). Though the Hasmonean struggle for autonomy against the Seleucids would continue for twenty more years, the era of the Antiochene persecutions had come to an end. The writing of apocalypses, however, had not.

We have already noted that Daniel and contemporaneous Enochic texts arise in a time of significant crisis—that is, the Antiochene persecutions and the Maccabean revolt. Responding to a crisis is indeed a feature of many early Jewish apocalypses. For example, in the wake of the destruction of the second temple by the Romans in 70 CE, 4 Ezra and 2 Baruch return to the topic of the destruction of the first temple by the Babylonians in 586 BCE as a way to reflect on the new catastrophe.[23] Yet not all apocalypses are necessarily moored in some clear historical provocation. Sometimes apocalypses arise out of a general sense of unease, rather than a particular historical calamity. Robert Williamson Jr. and

21. Newsom, *Daniel: A Commentary*, 20.
22. Hayes and Mandell, *Jewish People in Classical Antiquity*, 13–59.
23. Sheinfeld, "Decline of Second Temple Jewish Apocalypticism."

Justin Jeffcoat Schedtler describe this sense as a dissonance, "a perceived lack of fit between the reality of lived existence and the way that people feel the world 'ought to be.'"[24] For the scribes behind the book of Daniel, this dissonance appears to be rooted in active persecution. For others, though, the uneasiness may be more of an internal perception or "general sense of wariness."[25]

Apocalypse Now

During the reign of Antiochus, life for many Jews in Judea went from complex to downright chaotic. The Daniel apocalypses emerged as the way of storytelling and sense-making that met the chaos of the moment. The apocalypse was an innovation not only in the realm of literary development but also in conceptualizing the way that God works in relationship to the powers of the world. It reframed the empire's narrative of domination to assert God's control over history and to pinpoint an end to the chaos and terror of the day.

We should not imagine that a solitary ancient Jewish scholar, facing a rising tide of political oppression, suddenly sat down at a desk one day and invented the first apocalypse out of whole cloth. Rather, a certain way of viewing the world crystallized around some experimental writings that, at least on an ancient and scribal scale, "went viral." To name the apocalypse as a distinctive genre is a matter of hindsight. Like the other dynamic phenomena we have observed in the Old Testament, the apocalypse built on existing traditions and grew out of shared experiences within the community.

Similarly, when it comes to connecting the development of apocalyptic literature with the life of the church today, we should not imagine that we can suddenly invent a new mode of communication

24. Williamson and Schedtler, "Apocalyptic Movements in Early Judaism," 100–101.
25. Williamson and Schedtler, "Apocalyptic Movements in Early Judaism," 110.

that will invigorate the church's communal identity in the midst of a hostile world. Instead, we are again prompted to tune our ears to the new ways of writing and framing, communicating and conceptualizing, that are rising within our communities to meet the current moment. But first, what is that moment? And is it analogous at all to the context of second-century BCE Judea?

The development of the apocalypse, like the popularity of the court stories, underscores the fact that much of the biblical literature reflects Judah's position as a conquered people surviving under a changing cast of imperial kings. This circumstance is decidedly *not* analogous to the state of the Christian church in the United States today. While the institutional church may be losing ground as a cultural and political influence, Christianity as a whole still has significant cultural and even political capital. Christianity remains the religious orientation of a majority of Americans, most of whom worship freely and without fear. When it comes to learning from the innovations of apocalyptic literature, we must be careful not simply to place today's actors in for the ancient characters.

Nevertheless, I am drawn to Portier-Young's observation that the ancient apocalypse "intervened in the logic of terror," because there are so many ways in which a *logic of terror* runs rampant in the world today. It is the logic of any totalizing system that holds sway by fear, convincing us that the only power in the world is its own. The logic of racism, ingrained like a cancer in our economic systems and social structures, teaches us to fear our neighbor and disdain difference. The logic of addiction narrows our hope, convincing us that only our drug of choice—be it a literal or a figurative one—has the power to free us. The logic of predatory capitalism teaches us that there are not enough resources to go around and that the freedom of the market is of a higher value than the well-being of our neighbor. Studying the Daniel apocalypses invites us first to *name the monsters* that terrorize our world.

You will think of other horrors to list, and new monsters are bound to emerge. After all, terror can be innovative, too, even in the Bible—just think of Pharaoh's command that the Hebrews, already trapped in the misery of slavery, must gather straw to make their bricks on top of their existing workload (Exod. 5). The creative energy humanity pours into inventing new methods of cruelty continues to astonish. Sometimes the monsters will be individual tyrants, but more often they will be systems—powers and principalities, ways of thinking and being and living in the world that rule by terror and claim total control. Sometimes our own theology may be the monster. Sometimes—maybe quite often—church participates in the logic of terror. When that happens, we must be willing to name that too.

Despite the odd and frightening imagery of Daniel, its symbolic language actually *clarifies* the identity and nature of the oppressor. The monsters are unmasked. Apocalypses are, after all, revelations, unveilings. In its apocalyptic visions Daniel invites the reader to look the horned beasts in the eye and recognize them for what they are: powerful but finite, terrible but limited. When the reader and the visionary coalesce around that shared knowledge, they are also empowered to imagine new ways of understanding God's ordering of the world. In this way, despite the novelty of the apocalypse genre, Daniel stands squarely in the line of the Israelite prophets, who imagined a future different from the present state of exploitation and oppression, a future in which God's own justice would be realized.[26]

We cannot know the degree to which the Daniel apocalypses were "successful" at resisting the totalizing narrative of Antiochus. We know the Maccabean revolt was successful at inaugurating Hasmonean rule in its day, but since Danielic resistance appears to be more about the internal persistence of individuals and the community in times of oppression, we are unable to

---

26. Brueggemann, *Prophetic Imagination*.

measure its effectiveness. As Portier-Young points out, the early Jewish apocalypses were interested in resistance *discourse* as a type of resistance action.[27] We do know, however, that the book was meaningful enough to be transmitted through generations, read in community, and eventually counted among the books we call canonical today. The apocalypse, then, can turn the church's attention not only to the way it relates functionally to the powers of the world but also to the ways that its discourse—its speech or rhetoric—can resist those powers (or else may inadvertently support them). What new genres—new ways of speaking, storytelling, and sense-making—are arising to articulate new and life-giving ways of moving through God's world?

Like so much of the Old Testament, the Daniel apocalypses should also give us pause when it comes to replicating their worldview. Unlike the tales that precede it, the latter half of Daniel is "zoomed out" almost as far as the camera lens can go. It takes a big-picture view of history, focusing on a long-term divine plan from epoch to epoch. As with any theology of divine providence, it can be easy to slip into an uncritical affirmation that everything that happens—including the acute suffering of the oppressed while the powerful flourish—is planned or desired by God. Those kinds of theological claims must be accompanied by careful reflection on the power dynamics involved in their declaration. It is one thing for a persecuted minority to claim God's providential hand in their own suffering; it is quite another thing for a person or group in power, removed from or even benefiting from another's suffering, to pronounce that God continues to allow that suffering for some greater purpose.

As a new genre to make meaning out of dissonances, apocalypse provided a powerful tool to a marginalized community, but it was a tool also accessible to the powerful and economically advantaged.[28] Apocalypses proclaim to have the key to knowledge of the

---

27. Portier-Young, *Apocalypse against Empire*, 44–45.
28. Williamson and Schedtler, *Apocalyptic Movements in Early Judaism*, 100–110.

one true reality of the world. For people experiencing persecution, that kind of truth claim is a compelling tool of resistance. In the hands of a charismatic autocrat, those kinds of claims can wreak great havoc on a faith community, meeting one kind of tyranny with another. Apocalypses turn our attention to the way power operates in the world, but we must engage these questions with wariness and with humility.

By devoting their attention to the grand sweep of public history, the Daniel apocalypses also tend to ignore the everyday lives of people on the ground. Newsom observes, "Apocalyptic, as it is represented in Daniel, has no way of valuing or even conceiving of time as it is shaped by the daily routine of preparing meals, feeding and changing a baby, or planting and harvesting a garden. . . . Many of the most important events in history do not take place on the world stage but in the politics of everyday life, as women and men engage in local struggles for justice and compassion."[29] The Daniel apocalypses draw our attention to power writ large, and we must not ignore the influence that the church's patterns of speech and action can have on those powers, either to shore them up or to push back against them. Nevertheless, if we look only at the broad sweep of time, we may miss the small moments every day in which the church—which is to say, the body of Christ—can testify to the ongoing faithfulness of God, day in and day out, in the midst of a rapidly changing world.

---

29. Newsom, "Daniel," 298.

5

Biblical Foundations for Creative Change

According to the book of Ezra, sometime around 535 BCE the community of Israelites in Judah gathered to lay the foundation of the second Jerusalem temple. The first temple had been destroyed in 586 BCE by the Babylonians, who had besieged the city, captured Judah's king, and sent into exile the nation's elites, some of whom were forced into servitude under their foreign rulers.

The fall of Jerusalem shook the foundations of Israel's faith. God's promises to David of an eternal kingdom seemed broken, and the ruins of the temple—understood to be God's dwelling place—led even the most faithful Israelites to question whether God had abandoned God's people altogether. But then, in 539 BCE, King Cyrus of Persia defeated Babylon and instructed the exiles to return to Judah and rebuild the Jerusalem temple. Israelites whose parents or grandparents had been expelled from the land during the Babylonian exile began to return in waves to Judah. Hope surged.

Jeshua, the high priest, and Zerubbabel, the governor, began rebuilding the life of corporate worship in Judah by setting up the altar for burnt offerings and observing the festival calendar. Eventually they procured supplies to begin construction on the temple itself. Like many ground-breaking and ribbon-cutting ceremonies today, the laying of the foundation was accompanied by a festive atmosphere with certain ritual observances. The book of Ezra describes the scene:

> When the builders laid the foundation of the temple of the LORD, the priests in their vestments were stationed to praise the LORD with trumpets, and the Levites, the sons of Asaph, with cymbals, according to the directions of King David of Israel; and they sang responsively, praising and giving thanks to the LORD,
>
> > "For he is good,
> > for his steadfast love endures forever toward Israel."
>
> And all the people responded with a great shout when they praised the LORD, because the foundation of the house of the LORD was laid. But many of the priests and Levites and heads of families, old people who had seen the first house on its foundations, wept with a loud voice when they saw this house, though many shouted aloud for joy, so that the people could not distinguish the sound of the joyful shout from the sound of the people's weeping, for the people shouted so loudly that the sound was heard far away. (Ezra 3:10–13)

Rising together in this remarkable scene are joyful shouts praising God for newness as well as sorrowful cries grieving the loss of the old. Past and present, tradition and innovation, old and new, sadness and hope, grief and possibility—all of these dualities collide here, amid the dust of the first temple and the foundation blocks of the second, like so many energized atoms.

I can think of no more poignant picture of what change looks like than this image of the commencement of the second temple's construction. Sounds of loss and of promise mingle indistinguishably. This vivid and moving scene alone is enough to commend the Old Testament to us for further reflection on what it might offer the future of the church.

Yet as I have tried to show throughout this book, the Old Testament is valuable not only for the words on its pages but also for the processes and predicaments that birthed it. And it is in the period depicted in this very scene—the era of the return to Judah under Persian domination—that many biblical texts crystallized, including the Pentateuch and the final edition of the Deuteronomistic History.[1] When the scribes, priests, and other elites—or, more likely, their children and grandchildren—returned to Judah from exile in Babylon, they found there people who had never left as well as people who had been resettled there from elsewhere, many of whom were also worshipers of Yahweh. The community had to renegotiate who its authorities were, adding into the mix the Persian leadership that now exercised imperial control over the land and its people. Judah reckoned with intra-community fractures as well as external pressures.[2] All these circumstances characterize the post-exilic experience. It was a time of crisis and change for religious communities seeking to be faithful to God. The world from which the Hebrew Bible emerged was extraordinarily complex. It was never easy, straightforward, or obvious, and neither are the texts it birthed. Faced with enormous cultural, political, and theological upheaval, the Bible's storytellers and poets found innovative ways to give voice to the ongoing relationship between Israel and its God.

Having taken a whirlwind tour through several of the Bible's dynamic innovations, it is time to return again to the question with which our study began: *Why is that important for the church?*

---

1. Cf. Ska, *Introduction to Reading the Pentateuch*, 184–216; Römer, *So-Called Deuteronomistic History*, 165–83.

2. Ezra-Nehemiah recounts aggressive opposition to both the temple- and the wall-building efforts, difficulties with local authorities acting on behalf of Persia, and intra-community conflict over economics and intermarriage.

In the opening chapter I called for understanding the encounter between reader and text as an atomic particle collision, where the text and the reader, energized by the Holy Spirit, crash together in a generative, light-filled, creative burst. I argued that the Old Testament itself is as dynamic as its readers, exhibiting multiplicity in the cultural contexts that influenced it, the types of texts it contains, the historical eras from which it arises, the authorial and editorial hands that formed it, and the perspectives it represents. I claimed that the insights unearthed by critical biblical scholarship, which can sometimes seem irrelevant to the daily tasks of pastoral leadership and congregational mission, can actually contribute new hope to the work of church renewal. By embracing the Bible's dynamic witness, we recognize that the texts of the Bible arose in times of cultural, political, social, and even theological upheaval—times that were, much like our own era, full of complexity and uncertainty.

Through chapters 2, 3, and 4, we investigated texts and traditions from across the Hebrew Scriptures that exhibit various modes of innovation. In chapter 2 we saw how the creation and flood stories of Genesis and the court stories of Daniel, Esther, and Joseph adapt the popular literary culture of their day, revamping existing genres to make particular claims about the God of Israel and about life in Diaspora. I proposed that those texts should prompt faith communities to be both intentional and reflective about how they engage with the world around them and to consider what the stories of their communities are, how they are told, and whom they exclude or include.

In chapter 3 we looked closely at two examples of theological innovation, seeing how, at pivotal points in the history of Israel, the books of Deuteronomy and Ezekiel reconsider how the community encounters God. In the case of Deuteronomy, literary development had a direct effect on the lived experiences of everyday Israelites, as worship shifted away from local shrines and toward the central sanctuary in Jerusalem. For the prophet Ezekiel, the

Babylonian exile forced him to consider how God might be both present in and absent from Jerusalem and Babylon. We noted that both of these texts show dynamic engagement with core concepts of the relationship between God and Israel, and yet these reconsiderations happen within a particular social matrix that is not likely to represent the entire community. Thus the same texts that showcase theological innovation also remind us that our own identities and experiences are never absent from our interpretations.

Lastly, we returned to the book of Daniel to focus on its apocalyptic final chapters, observing that the crisis of the Antiochene persecutions was met by the flourishing of a new genre. Though apocalyptic imagery may seem impenetrable now, in its day it clarified for its readers the identity of the oppressors and the promise of God's ultimate victory over them. I proposed that apocalypses prompt us to unmask the monsters of church and world today and to be on the lookout for radically new ways to articulate God's promises for creation.

On Critical Biblical Scholarship

A seminary degree is not a requirement for reading the Bible faithfully. We know this already, but it bears reaffirming. Each of us is equipped by the Holy Spirit to interpret the Bible ourselves and to be transformed by the living Word of God. My call for integrating the insights of critical biblical scholarship more robustly into the life, work, and future of the church is decidedly *not* a rejection of lay readings, a call for all Christians to receive advanced biblical studies training, or an assertion that only "experts" can read the Bible "correctly." I have emphasized throughout that there is no such thing as the "correct meaning" of *any* given biblical text. Instead, the Old Testament is a place where the dynamic text and its equally dynamic readers encounter one another, generating newness. The Holy Spirit is ultimately the energizing force in this encounter, and no one is excluded from the Spirit's reach.

At the same time, I contend that the church should not regard biblical criticism as merely an interesting intellectual exercise, as an informative but ultimately backgrounded part of sermon exegesis, or as something that must be siloed away from the life, work, and faith of Christian communities. To be sure, there are times when those silos can be appropriate. I hope it would go without saying that just as a Christian reader need not be an academic, so, too, one need not be Christian—or Jewish or a person of any faith—to read the Bible fruitfully or to contribute robustly to the field. Moreover, no one, including me, wants to sit through a lecture on source criticism of Genesis as part of a worship service. Nevertheless, confessional interests and biblical scholarship have historically been deeply enmeshed with each other, at least within seminaries and religiously affiliated universities.[3] Much of critical biblical scholarship has been driven by people of faith seeking answers to theologically oriented questions. We have often faltered, however, in translating that work for the everyday life of the church.

Some of the examples of dynamic biblical innovation we have explored belong to what is usually called the "historical-critical method" of biblical interpretation, which is interested in diachronic readings: how a text formed over time. This category especially applies to source criticism of the Pentateuch, which we investigated with regard to the creation and flood stories in Genesis and the relationship between the Covenant Code in Exodus and the book of Deuteronomy. Other parts of our study, though, saw critical readings illuminate the impact of other ancient Near Eastern literature on the Bible's literary style. We investigated the political and theological circumstances that are reflected in the text and also some that lurked behind it during its composition. We looked at texts in their constituent parts and also as wholes and as part of larger literary and historical conglomerations. In other

3. See Barton, *Nature of Biblical Criticism*, 164–71.

words, biblical scholarship does not unravel texts into unreadable pieces; instead, it pieces together a fuller picture than what is available on the surface. Critical biblical scholarship offers the church *more*, not *less*.

So what distinguishes a "critical" from an "uncritical" reading? John Barton offers this helpful reflection:

> What, then, is biblical criticism? It is an inquiry into the biblical text that takes its starting point from the attempt to understand, a desire to read the text in its coherence and to grasp its drift. This is essentially a literary operation. Unlike precritical and some postcritical interpreters, however, biblical critics do not assume that all texts can in fact successfully be read in this holistic way, but are *prepared to encounter frustrations in reading*. Such frustrations meet noncritical interpreters, too, in the form of inconsistencies and irregularities in the text which on the face of it thwart the attempt at holistic reading. When this happens, noncritical and critical interpreters diverge in their approach. Noncritical readers take the givenness (whether religious or literary) of the text to authorize or even demand harmonization, even if the result is to produce an "unreadable" (because unclassifiable) text. The critical response is to ask about the genre of the text, and on the basis of the answer to decide how the inconsistencies are to be regarded.[4]

My concern for the church is that we often fail to notice—or, upon noticing, fail to engage—these literary frustrations. Even readers who are untroubled by textual dissonances will often opt for a surface engagement with a smaller snippet of verses rather than tackling the diachronic or otherwise deeper textual issues that lurk behind it. Of course, we in the guild of theological biblical

---

4. Barton, *Nature of Biblical Criticism*, 30 (emphasis added). Barton argues that biblical criticism is primarily a literary endeavor, assessing and reassessing genre toward the goal of comprehension, rather than a historical project. Ultimately, I agree with his appraisal, though I am less sanguine about the possibility that such a thing as what he calls the "plain sense" can ever be pinpointed.

scholarship are as much to blame or more for failing to make these kinds of connections meaningful for everyday readers. This book is one small offering toward remedying that lapse.

One impulse toward resolving, rather than acknowledging, dissonances is to "harmonize" them. Harmonization tries to explain how inner-biblical contradictions are not, in fact, contradictions. This phenomenon is already present within the biblical canon.[5] The book of Chronicles is a post-exilic re-presentation of the monarchic history, using many of the same texts as Samuel and Kings but from a distinctive perspective that gives particular attention to the righteousness of David, the work of the temple and its functionaries, and the role of prophets. In chapter 3 we saw how Deuteronomy revises earlier legal tradition to call for centralization of worship, which involved the concomitant revision of the Passover festival from an in-home celebration to a pilgrimage one. Second Kings 23:21–23 notes that Josiah celebrated a Deuteronomic Passover in Jerusalem as part of his program of religious reforms. When Chronicles gives an account of Josiah's Passover, it does not offer merely a mention of it as 2 Kings does but instead gives a detailed report of how the celebration is conducted. Describing the preparation of the Passover lamb, Chronicles reports, "They boiled the Passover lamb with fire [*waybashelu happesakh ba'esh*] according to the ordinance" (2 Chron. 35:13a AT). This peculiar construction—to boil with fire—reflects parts of the Passover regulations in both Exodus and Deuteronomy. Exodus 12:8–9 instructs the Israelites to roast the lamb over fire (*tseli-'esh*), but Deuteronomy 16:7a says, "You shall boil [*bishalta*] it and eat it at the place the LORD your God will choose" (AT). Chronicles appears to use a mash-up of the two regulations to come up with the new, if physically impossible, way to describe the cooking of the lamb.

5. The following example from 2 Chronicles is from Barton, *Nature of Biblical Criticism*, 20–21, which is itself in conversation with Sommer, "Inner-biblical Interpretation." For a fuller analysis of the development of the Passover traditions, see Levinson, *Deuteronomy and the Hermeneutics of Legal Innovation*, 53–97.

I suppose we could call harmonization an innovation of sorts. But it strikes me that making this kind of adjustment in our interpretations is more an impulse to hold on to everything old, leading to an interpretation that is more "unreadable" (to use Barton's word) than the dissonances that precipitated the interpretation. This impulse is a bit ironic in Chronicles, since the book is a representation of the monarchic history from Samuel and Kings with a particular agenda, which lifts up David and Solomon, the work of the priests and Levites, and the temple. For example, Chronicles reveals few of the more sordid accounts of David's life; there is no mention of his rape of Bathsheba and his arranging the murder of her husband, Uriah (2 Sam. 11–12). On the one hand, Chronicles represents part of the Bible's multivocity, yet on the other, at least in this particular example, it also tries to harmonize older ideas instead of letting them stand together. The desire to make "the rough places a plain," to borrow a phrase from Isaiah, is understandable and probably on occasion warranted. My hope, though, is that lingering in the discomfort of the rough places will help us exercise new muscles for interpretation, ones that leave us strengthened to face the complexity of the life of faith in the midst of rapid change.

Biblical Principles for Creative Change

I offer the following "biblical principles for creative change" with some hesitancy because, as I have already noted, the Bible provides no universal road map for church renewal—nor, I would venture, does it offer such a map for just about anything. The Old Testament is more like a set of painted landscapes than a list of directions. These offerings are less "principles" and more gestures or prompts—embers for igniting your own imagination about what newness these learnings can inspire for your particular context. Though I have referred throughout this book to "the church," that term (not unlike "the Bible") obscures the wonderfully diverse, yet often unfortunately fractious, state of Christianity today. Different individual churches, as well as different traditions within the church universal, will face different needs, and so any of these prompts must be adapted accordingly.

Be a Creative Storyteller

We know the Bible is full of magnificent stories. We have learned from our explorations of Genesis and Daniel just how creative those stories are. Some biblical narratives borrow from existing popular genres and give them their own twist. We saw that the apocalypse, while echoing prophecy and other eschatological traditions, is nonetheless a new type of literature that emerges in Second Temple Judaism and particularly flourishes under the stress of the Antiochene persecutions. While the core relationship between God and Israel stays constant, the new circumstances of new days require new stories, and new means of storytelling, for understanding and conveying that relationship.

Embracing creativity in storytelling may involve technical innovations, such as utilizing new media. But it may also mean embracing *new stories*—new ways of understanding the identity of your community. I once belonged to a wonderful church that had gone from over two thousand members in the 1940s to somewhere around four hundred members in the early 2000s. Their identity was rooted in those old "glory days," if glory can be understood in terms of membership numbers. Thus the story of the church was stuck in nostalgia and pain—it was the emptiest big church in town. But the church's mission and ministries were vibrant, serving the community with generosity and joy. The church found a new wind in its sails when it began to change its narrative to talk about itself as the most missionally focused small church in town—that just happened to be in a big building. Stories need to be updated to reflect the changing shape of any community. As we have seen, updating stories is a fundamental biblical idea.

A popular idea in many Christian circles today is to talk about the Bible as "God's story." This idea proliferates in both mainline and evangelical traditions. For example, Luther Seminary publishes a "Narrative Lectionary," which arranges texts "in a narrative sequence to help people see Scripture as a story that has coherence and a dynamic movement."[6] Zondervan produces an edition of the Bible called *The Story: The Bible as One Continuing Story of God and His People*, described as "an abridged, chronological Bible that reads like a novel."[7] These are just two representative examples of the way that the concept of God's story accomplishes creative storytelling. It makes what can sometimes seem like a jumble of unrelated texts easier to understand by emphasizing a coherent, overarching narrative. It turns people's attention to texts they might otherwise ignore. It draws important lines of continuity across the testaments, and it makes connections between disparate pieces of Scripture to articulate the gospel message with clarity and cohesion. As a theological idea, it is brilliantly compelling.

Nevertheless, as a representation of the Bible, the notion of "God's story" is also significantly limiting. Flattening the Bible into a single narrative may obscure some of its vexing difficulties, but it also risks fitting the Bible into what kind of book we would rather it be, instead of the kind of book it is. The Bible is a book—and a collection of books—that surfaces competing ancient ideologies, often without resolving them. As we have seen, not all the constitutive parts of the Bible are, in fact, story. To focus on a biblical metanarrative will inevitably mean prioritizing the narrative portions of Scripture over poetry, law, and other genres or else reshaping those different genres into more linear forms.

I believe this flattening is particularly perilous when it obscures biblical poetry. Poetry itself can be narrative, of course,

6. "Narrative Lectionary FAQ," Working Preacher, https://www.workingpreacher.org/narrative_faqs.aspx.
7. "What Is the Story?," Zondervan, https://www.thestory.com/what-is-the-story.

conveying the passage of time and telling a story through verse rather than prose. But there is very little narrative poetry in the Old Testament.[8] Instead, biblical poetry tends toward the lyrical, the descriptive, and the prophetic. This kind of poetry does not fit neatly into a story. Instead, it bursts out of the bounds of reason and respectability and imagines what prose cannot. The Bible's poetic texts are among its most dynamic, in that they so readily defy attempts to pin down their meaning. Metaphors can attest simultaneously to God's ferocity and God's tenderness.[9] Poems testify with vivid language to God's power, love, and fidelity:

> At the blast of your nostrils the waters piled up,
>   the floods stood up in a heap;
>   the deeps congealed in the heart of the sea. (Exod. 15:8)

Poems call up visions of an almost inconceivable future—when "nation shall not lift sword up against nation" (Isa. 2:4) and when "the wolf and the lamb shall feed together" (65:25). Of course, narrative does not preclude using vivid imagery, but the cumulative effect of poetic devices is to "show" rather than "tell," as the saying goes.

In an Advent sermon on Isaiah 11:1–9, Walter Brueggemann describes the generativity of poetry: "Poetry will break the claims of the memo. Poetry will open the world beyond reason. Poetry will give access to contradictions and tensions that logic must deny. Poetry will not only remember; it will propose and conjure and wonder and imagine and foretell."[10] Telling the Bible as a story risks wrestling its poetic texts into a linear, controllable form, when poetry inherently resists such strictures. The evocative pos-

---

8. The "Song of the Sea" in Exodus 15:1–18 and "Deborah's Song" in Judges 5:1–31 can be classified as narrative poems. Both are among the oldest texts in the Hebrew Bible, and both celebrate victory in battle.

9. Brettler, "Incompatible Metaphors for YHWH in Isaiah 40–66."

10. Brueggemann, "Poem," in *Collected Sermons*, 2:9.

sibilities for the future that poetry describes are the kind of bold imaginings the church needs. Creative storytelling rooted in the dynamism of the Old Testament will need to tell a story for the future, not just recount the past. It may be that the best way to tell that story of the future is not, in fact, with stories but with the lyrical, logic-busting, boundary-breaking promise of poetry.

Ellen Davis has advocated for reading all of Scripture, regardless of genre, as if it were poetry, because poetry requires slow and attentive reading, often for the sake of delight rather than some sense of usefulness. She writes, "On the whole, it is better to think of the Bible as poetry rather than as prose, at least as we generally distinguish between those two in our reading practices. You cannot skim poetry for plot, and you cannot read it in distraction. That is why poetry is read by poetry lovers: it is a nonutilitarian act, like many other acts of love."[11] Though it may seem that I have advocated in this book for how to make the insights of critical biblical scholarship more "useful" for the church, I am more inclined to lean into some of that nonutilitarian delight. By giving the Old Testament our full attention, we can recognize, and revel in, its dissonances.

Recognize and Celebrate Difference

The Old Testament is built on particularity: it is concerned first and foremost with the descendants of Jacob, who is renamed Israel and fathers a nation. The covenant with Jacob's grandfather Abraham proclaims that "in you all the families of the earth shall be blessed" (Gen. 12:3b), but Abraham's family remains the center of that promise. The Hebrew Bible presents a particular people in covenant relationship with the God Yahweh, and it calls for unfailing allegiance to that God. The texts emphasize that it is Israel whom Yahweh chooses to liberate from the bondage of Pharaoh, it is Israel whom Yahweh chooses to occupy the land

11. Davis, "Soil That Is Scripture," 41.

of Canaan, and it is David and his descendants whom Yahweh chooses to reign in Jerusalem. At the heart of the Hebrew Bible is the unique and particular relationship between God and Israel.

Beyond this steady core, some texts exhibit a more aggressive particularity, while others show a more expansive outlook. The Deuteronomistic History, for example, displays a fierce polemic against "foreign women," claiming that they turn the heads of Israelite men toward the worship of foreign gods, leading to the rampant apostasies that, in Deuteronomic thought, break the stipulations of the covenant and lead to exile.[12] Ezra-Nehemiah picks up that thread, narrating the community's potential expulsion of the non-Israelite wives of Israelite men, along with their children (Ezra 9–10; cf. Neh. 13:23–31). Yet the book of Ruth tells the story of a heroic Moabite woman who shows fidelity to the God of Israel and becomes the great-grandmother of David. Isaiah 56:7 presents God's declaration that "my house shall be called a house of prayer for all peoples."

If we were to ask "What does the Old Testament say about difference?" we would come up with many, sometimes divergent answers based on how the texts contained within it speak to that theme. However, if we reshape our question into "Where can we observe difference in the Old Testament?" then perhaps we can be prompted to push our investigation beyond the theme of difference as related only to people or groups—or beyond a narrow focus on one passage at a time. Then we are better positioned to observe that Ezra-Nehemiah and Ruth exist together, products of the same core relationship but reverberating unresolved through the canon. Then the sources that constitute the Pentateuch become less of an obstacle that impedes a smooth reading and more a part of the intrinsic diversity in the authoritative witness of Scripture. What would it look like to embrace multivalence, allowing diversity rather than dogmatism in our interpretations to become our

---

12. For more on that polemic, see Howard, "1 and 2 Kings."

authoritative norm? In a world that is fractured and polarized, is there a way this positive persistence of different perspectives in our textual tradition can spill over into our churches and our communities?

This attention to and embrace of difference should not imply that life does not often require adjudication between texts. We should also ask ourselves, "Where can we observe uniformity—or inflexibility or attempts at erasure—in the Old Testament?" Holding on to different outlooks is no excuse for perpetuating harm. Nor should we imagine that there has been no erasure of traditions in the composition and compilation of Scripture. We have a selection of perspectives that are different from one another, but those perspectives are largely limited to those from the scribal class who had access to writing materials, literacy training, and the centers of learning that preserved the tradition. Yet even within those strictures, a remarkable diversity of perspectives is intrinsic to the nature of the Old Testament. Considered within the dynamics of churches today, it can prompt us to think about how we hold difference—of people, of ideas, of perspectives—in our communities.

Listen for New and Previously Unheard Voices

As I have just emphasized with regard to difference, the Old Testament is multivocal: it reflects the concerns of different people or groups within ancient Israel as well as the issues relevant to different eras or circumstances in ancient Israel's history. The Old Testament hosts encounters between different voices, sometimes within the texts themselves but often concealed behind their words. In addition to turning our attention to the differences hosted within the Old Testament, this characteristic can also prompt us to ask, "Whose voices does our community lift up?" The related, unavoidable, and more important question is, of course, "Whose voices are left out?"

The Old Testament may be multivocal, but it is certainly not *omnivocal*; it does not transmit every voice or every idea, even though it does preserve contrasting ones. Within the text, the voices of women are scantly represented, and it is unlikely that women authored much, if any, of the Bible.[13] We noted that the Babylonian exile signaled a monumental change for the life and work of the scribal class that was deported, but what of the people left in the land, "the poorest people of the land [left] to be vinedressers and tillers of the soil" (2 Kings 25:12)? We do not know what their experiences of the fall of Jerusalem were. By emphasizing the Bible's dynamism, I do not mean to lift it up as a model of egalitarian discourse. Nor does attending to its dynamism erase any of its problematic passages. Rather, the presence of this imperfectly multivocal phenomenon in the text should tune our ears to the voices—and their absence—in our churches and faith communities. Where do we welcome otherness, and where have we attempted to overwrite it?

Embrace Uncertainty

"What does this text mean?" "Why is that story in the Bible?" "What are we supposed to *do* with this passage?" These are all questions that pop up in readers' encounters with the Bible, whether in worship, a Bible study, a confirmation class, or a graduate seminar. Reading the Bible can sometimes leave us more puzzled than enlightened, asking more questions instead of finding all the answers we were looking for. In times of complexity or crisis, it is tempting to look for easy answers or at least abandon our search when we encounter tough ones. The more the ground moves underneath my feet, the more inclined I am to stick to smooth, flat terrain.

Yet I am comforted by the fact that the answers have *never* been easy. The layers of interpretation and reinterpretation we can

13. For an example of critical biblical interpretation that listens for and amplifies the Bible's marginalized voices, see Gafney, *Womanist Midrash*.

see behind the texts of the Old Testament testify to a tradition that opens itself to reflection and re-examination. When we read accounts of God appearing either directly or via messenger to Abraham, Hagar, Moses, and others, it can be tempting to think that experiences of God in the biblical era were all in-person, clear, and unambiguous and to bemoan what seems like God's distance from us today. Yet even when we accept each of those accounts at face value, the texts where God's presence is backgrounded rather than foregrounded are equally numerous. Think, for example, of the Joseph story (Gen. 37–50), in which God is understood to be active in Joseph's fate, but God does not appear as a character in the story—certainly not in the same way as God appears in the Abraham narratives. Or consider the book of Esther, where God is only a hint, a suggestion; God does not appear and is never named in the text. Coupling the evidence in the text with the development of biblical texts and traditions illustrates that uncertainty accompanied our ancestors in the faith as much as it attends us. The Bible does not necessarily provide every answer, but it walks with us in our questions. And that is good news.

Epilogue

A Note on the New Testament

This is a book about the Old Testament. I have deliberately avoided engaging material from the New Testament so that we might hear the Old Testament speaking on its own terms first. But questions nonetheless hover over this self-consciously Christian reading: What about the New Testament? Is it an innovation? Does it display the same dynamism as the Old Testament?

The "new" in "New Testament" predisposes us to look for what makes it different—even innovative—compared with the Hebrew Bible. Certainly the Jesus movement brings to the already diverse world of Second Temple Judaism some new theological ideas, including naming Jesus of Nazareth as the Messiah.[1] But when it comes to textual dynamism, the New Testament is in many ways a continuation of the Old. The New Testament is certainly multivocal: the four Gospels provide front-and-center evidence for this. Despite the overlap in core texts, each of the four Gospels puts its own distinctive spin on its presentation of the life and ministry of Jesus. The Deutero-Pauline letters also represent literary

1. On the diversity of Second Temple Judaism, see Hayes and Mandell, *Jewish People in Classical Antiquity*, 84–93; Grabbe, *Introduction to Second Temple Judaism*.

dynamism in the New Testament: Ephesians, Colossians, 2 Thessalonians, 1 and 2 Timothy, and Titus all claim to be written by Paul, but New Testament scholars generally agree that these were written by other people, introducing new voices in the guise of an existing authority.[2] The Epistle genre itself is also introduced to the canon in the New Testament. While there is certainly nothing new about writing letters, there are no stand-alone epistolary books in the Hebrew Bible.[3]

This continuity between the testaments is particularly important to acknowledge, because Jesus is often employed as a kind of trump card against the Old Testament, in lieu of wrestling with its more difficult points. Of course, reading the Old Testament through the lens of the revelation of Jesus Christ is an important part of a Christian hermeneutic. At the same time, Christian tradition affirms the authority of both the Old and the New Testaments. To say "It's a good thing we have Jesus" when we encounter some of the Hebrew Bible's dissonances deprives us of an opportunity to wrestle with Scripture in all its fullness—to acknowledge that the Old Testament's dynamism offers us more, not less, and enrichment, not threat. Rather than meeting the Old Testament with a "But Jesus . . . ," I encourage Christians to meet it with "*And* Jesus . . ."

2. For more on the basics of New Testament authorship, see Smith and Kim, *Toward Decentering the New Testament*. Smith and Kim affirm for the New Testament many of the same ideas I have highlighted in the Old Testament. See, for example, their reflection on the multivocity of the Gospels: "Each Gospel should be respected as reflecting the author's literary and theological agenda or objective, his attempt to narrate the life, ministry, and death of Jesus from his perspective with the use of sources. Again, readers should resist the temptation to harmonize the Gospels. Differences may reflect the context or community to which each writer belonged, as well as their individual perspectives. Thus, differences among them also demonstrate that early believers in Jesus as God's Messiah or the Christ interpreted the events and people surrounding Jesus and his life, ministry, and death differently" (82).

3. There are several letters interpolated into the book of Ezra, and multiple texts, including 1 and 2 Kings, Jeremiah, and Esther, refer to the act of writing letters. The Letter of Jeremiah is a book of the Apocrypha. However, there is no clear parallel to the Epistle genre represented in the Hebrew Bible.

A Postscript on Praxis

In summer 1968 my grandfather, a Presbyterian minister, participated in a pulpit exchange with Newhaven Church in Edinburgh, Scotland. He and his family lived in the manse, and he preached the Sunday services and cared for the members of the Edinburgh congregation while his Church of Scotland counterpart did the same in Mebane, North Carolina. Fifty-one years later, my husband, Cader, also a Presbyterian minister, visited the same Edinburgh church on a summer sabbatical study leave. What he found there were the fruits of the theological reconsideration of holy space that had revitalized a struggling congregation.

Like so many churches in Europe at the end of the twentieth century, the Newhaven Church endured a steady decline in membership and financial support. They responded to that crisis with creativity and not a small amount of daring. They converted their multistory sanctuary into condominiums and then used the income from that project to renovate the church's lower level, which once served as its fellowship hall. Now that space is Newhaven Connections Café, a café run by the church, staffed primarily by church volunteers, that serves delicious and very affordable food and provides a significant source of income for the church itself.[4] One end of the hall provides flexible sanctuary space for Sunday services but can also serve as overflow seating for the café. The rest of the hall includes café tables and a commercial kitchen. On the weekday Cader visited, the café was bustling with young parents' groups and had clearly become a vibrant community gathering place. Neither pulpit nor cross was visible, but he will readily testify that God was present there.

I don't know the process by which Newhaven Church decided to take such an enormous leap of faith to pivot from the traditional pulpit my grandfather once filled to the basement ministry

4. More information about Newhaven Church and the Newhaven Connections Café can be found at the church's website: https://n-c.org.uk.

of food, gathering, and community building they now provide. My relationship with the church is only as an interested outside observer. But I do know that a willingness to radically reevaluate the mission of a faith community, to rethink which holy spaces God inhabits (and how), and to engage with the surrounding culture to tell a new story for a new day are all values identifiable in the Old Testament. Those values may indeed be noticeable on a surface reading of some texts, but it is in the backgrounds, cracks, and crevices where remarkable new strategies can be detected, revealing that innovation is a biblical value. The faithful people who shaped our sacred texts lived in turbulent times. They worked boldly and creatively to reckon with the changes that befell them and to continue to testify to God's ongoing covenant relationship with them in the midst of great uncertainty. We have much to learn not only from the words they wrote but also from the struggles that gave life to those words.

Bibliography

Barton, John. *The Nature of Biblical Criticism*. Louisville: Westminster John Knox, 2007.

———. *Reading the Old Testament: Method in Biblical Study*. Louisville: Westminster John Knox, 1996.

Borowski, Oded. *Every Living Thing: Daily Use of Animals in Ancient Israel*. Walnut Creek, CA: AltaMira, 1998.

Brettler, Mark Zvi. "Incompatible Metaphors for YHWH in Isaiah 40–66." *Journal for the Study of the Old Testament* 78 (1998): 97–120.

Brown, William P. *A Handbook to Old Testament Exegesis*. Louisville: Westminster John Knox, 2017.

Brueggemann, Walter. *Inscribing the Text: Sermons and Prayers of Walter Brueggemann*. Edited by Anna Carter Florence. Minneapolis: Fortress, 2004.

———. "The Poem: Subversion and Summons." In *The Collected Sermons of Walter Brueggemann*, 2:9–13. Louisville: Westminster John Knox, 2015.

———. *The Prophetic Imagination*. 40th anniversary ed. Minneapolis: Fortress, 2018.

Caputo, John D. *Hermeneutics: Facts and Interpretation in the Age of Information*. London: Pelican, 2018.

Charlesworth, James H., ed. *The Old Testament Pseudepigrapha*. 2 vols. Garden City, NY: Doubleday, 1985.

Collins, John J. *The Apocalyptic Imagination: An Introduction to Jewish Apocalyptic Literature*. 3rd ed. Grand Rapids: Eerdmans, 2016.

———. *Daniel*. Hermeneia. Minneapolis: Fortress, 1993.

———. "What Is Apocalyptic Literature?" In *The Oxford Handbook of Apocalyptic Literature*, edited by John J. Collins, 1–16. New York: Oxford University Press, 2014.

Cook, Stephen L. "Ezekiel." In *Theological Bible Commentary*, edited by Gail R. O'Day and David L. Petersen, 241–56. Louisville: Westminster John Knox, 2009.

Dalley, Stephanie. *Myths from Mesopotamia: Creation, the Flood, Gilgamesh, and Others*. Oxford: Oxford University Press, 1991.

Darr, Katheryn Pfisterer. *The Book of Ezekiel: Introduction, Commentary, and Reflections*. In *Introduction to Prophetic Literature, Isaiah, Jeremiah, Baruch, Letter of Jeremiah, Lamentations, Ezekiel*. Vol. 6 of New Interpreter's Bible, edited by Leander E. Keck, 1075–607. Nashville: Abingdon, 2001.

Davis, Ellen F. "The Soil That Is Scripture." In *Engaging Biblical Authority*, edited by William P. Brown, 36–44. Louisville: Westminster John Knox, 2007.

Day, John. "Comparative Ancient Near Eastern Study: The Genesis Flood Narrative in Relation to Ancient Near Eastern Flood Accounts." In *Biblical Interpretation and Method: Essays in Honour of John Barton*, edited by Katharine J. Dell and Paul M. Joyce, 74–88. Oxford: Oxford University Press, 2013.

Fentress-Williams, Judy. "Exodus." In *The Africana Bible Commentary: Reading Israel's Scriptures from Africa and the African Diaspora*, edited by Hugh R. Page Jr., 80–88. Minneapolis: Fortress, 2010.

Friedman, Richard Elliott. *Who Wrote the Bible?* New York: HarperOne, 1997.

Gafney, Wilda C. *Womanist Midrash: A Reintroduction to the Women of the Torah and the Throne*. Louisville: Westminster John Knox, 2017.

Gignilliat, Mark S. *Reading Scripture Canonically: Theological Instincts for Old Testament Interpretation*. Grand Rapids: Baker Academic, 2019.

Grabbe, Lester. *An Introduction to Second Temple Judaism: History and Religion of the Jews in the Time of Nehemiah, the Maccabees, Hillel, and Jesus*. London: T&T Clark, 2010.

Hanson, Paul D. "Apocalypses and Apocalypticism: The Genre and Introductory Overview." In *The Anchor Bible Dictionary: A–C*, edited by David Noel Freedman, 1:279–82. New York: Doubleday, 1992.

Hayes, John H., and Sara R. Mandell. *The Jewish People in Classical Antiquity: From Alexander to Bar Kochba*. Louisville: Westminster John Knox, 1998.

Hays, Christopher B. *Hidden Riches: A Sourcebook for the Comparative Study of the Hebrew Bible and Ancient Near East*. Louisville: Westminster John Knox, 2014.

Howard, Cameron B. R. "1 and 2 Kings." In *Women's Bible Commentary*, edited by Carol A. Newsom, Sharon H. Ringe, and Jacqueline E. Lapsley, 164–79. Louisville: Westminster John Knox, 2012.

Humphreys, W. Lee. "A Lifestyle for Diaspora: A Study of the Tales of Esther and Daniel." *Journal of Biblical Literature* 92 (1973): 211–23.

Kim, Uriah Y. *Decolonizing Josiah: Toward a Postcolonial Reading of the Deuteronomistic History*. Sheffield: Sheffield Phoenix, 2005.

Kutsko, John F. *Between Heaven and Earth: Divine Presence and Absence in the Book of Ezekiel*. Biblical and Judaic Studies 7. Winona Lake, IN: Eisenbrauns, 2000.

Levenson, Jon D. "Zion Traditions." In *The Anchor Bible Dictionary: Si–Z*, edited by David Noel Freedman, 6:1098–102. New York: Doubleday, 1992.

Levinson, Bernard M. *Deuteronomy and the Hermeneutics of Legal Innovation*. New York: Oxford University Press, 1997.

Lindenberger, J. M. "Ahiqar: A New Translation and Introduction." In *The Old Testament Pseudepigrapha*, vol. 2, edited by James H. Charlesworth, 479–507. Garden City, NY: Doubleday, 1985.

Longman, Tremper, III. "Proverbs." *Bible Odyssey*. http://www.bibleodyssey.org/tools/ask-a-scholar/proverbs.

Meyers, Carol. "Women's Religious Life in Ancient Israel." In *Women's Bible Commentary*, edited by Carol A. Newsom, Sharon H. Ringe, and Jacqueline E. Lapsley, 354–61. Louisville: Westminster John Knox, 2012.

Newsom, Carol A. "Daniel." In *Women's Bible Commentary*, edited by Carol A. Newsom, Sharon H. Ringe, and Jacqueline E. Lapsley, 293–98. Louisville: Westminster John Knox, 2012.

———. *Daniel: A Commentary*. Old Testament Library. Louisville: Westminster John Knox, 2014.

Nickelsburg, George W. E., and James C. VanderKam. *1 Enoch: A New Translation*. Minneapolis: Fortress, 2004.

Petersen, David L. *The Prophetic Literature: An Introduction*. Louisville: Westminster John Knox, 2002.

Portier-Young, Anathea E. *Apocalypse against Empire: Theologies of Resistance in Early Judaism*. Grand Rapids: Eerdmans, 2011.

Ramsey, George W. "Zadok." In *The Anchor Bible Dictionary: Si–Z*, edited by David Noel Freedman, 6:1034–36. New York: Doubleday, 1992.

Römer, Thomas. *The So-Called Deuteronomistic History: A Sociological, Historical and Literary Introduction*. London: T&T Clark, 2007.

Schniedewind, William M. *How the Bible Became a Book*. Cambridge: Cambridge University Press, 2004.

Schroeder, Fred E. H. *5000 Years of Popular Culture: Popular Culture before Printing*. Bowling Green, OH: Bowling Green University Popular Press, 1980.

Sheinfeld, Shayna. "The Decline of Second Temple Jewish Apocalypticism and the Rise of Rabbinic Judaism." In *Apocalypses in Context: Apocalyptic Currents through History*, edited by Kelly J. Murphy and Justin Jeffcoat Schedtler, 187–209. Minneapolis: Fortress, 2016.

Ska, Jean-Louis. *Introduction to Reading the Pentateuch*. Translated by Sr. Pascale Dominique. Winona Lake, IN: Eisenbrauns, 2006.

Smith, Mitzi J., and Yung Suk Kim. *Toward Decentering the New Testament: A Reintroduction*. Eugene, OR: Cascade Books, 2018.

Smith-Christopher, Daniel L. *The Book of Daniel: Introduction, Commentary, and Reflections*. In *Introduction to Apocalyptic Literature, Daniel, Additions to Daniel, Hosea, Joel, Amos, Obadiah, Jonah, Micah, Nahum, Habakkuk, Zephaniah, Haggai, Zechariah, Malachi*. Volume 7 of *New Interpreter's Bible*, edited by Leander Keck, 19–152. Nashville: Abingdon, 1996.

Sommer, Benjamin D. "Inner-biblical Interpretation." In *The Jewish Study Bible*, edited by Adele Berlin and Marc Zvi Brettler, 1829–34. Oxford: Oxford University Press, 2004.

Strawn, Brent A. *The Old Testament Is Dying: A Diagnosis and Recommended Treatment*. Grand Rapids: Baker Academic, 2017.

van der Toorn, Karel. *Scribal Culture and the Making of the Hebrew Bible*. Cambridge, MA: Harvard University Press, 2007.

Weissman Joselit, Jenna. *Set in Stone: America's Embrace of the Ten Commandments*. Oxford: Oxford University Press, 2017.

Williamson, Robert, Jr. *The Forgotten Books of the Bible: Recovering the Five Scrolls for Today*. Minneapolis: Fortress, 2018.

Williamson, Robert, Jr., and Justin Jeffcoat Schedtler. "Apocalyptic Movements in Early Judaism: Dissonance and Resistance." In *Apocalypses in Context: Apocalyptic Currents through History*, edited by Kelly J. Murphy and Justin Jeffcoat Schedtler, 87–111. Minneapolis: Fortress, 2016.

Wills, Lawrence M. *The Jew in the Court of the Foreign King: Ancient Jewish Court Legends*. Harvard Dissertations in Religion 26. Minneapolis: Fortress, 1990.

———. *The Jewish Novel in the Ancient World*. Ithaca, NY: Cornell University Press, 1995.

Scripture Index

Subject Index